THE
PENGUIN
PRINCIPLES

THE PENGUIN PRINCIPLES

A SURVIVAL MANUAL FOR CLERGY
SEEKING MATURITY IN MINISTRY

DAVID S. BELASIC
AND
PAUL M. SCHMIDT

Foreword by LYLE SCHALLER

THE PENGUIN PRINCIPLES

Copyright © 1986 by
The C.S.S. Publishing Company, Inc.
Lima, Ohio

Library of Congress Cataloging-in-Publication Data

Belasic, David S., 1935-
    The penguin principles.

    1. Pastoral theology. I. Schmidt, Paul M.,
1930-   II. Title.
BV4011.B42   1986   253'.2   85-15524
ISBN 0-89536-799-8

6817 / ISBN 0-89536-799-8   PRINTED IN U.S.A.

Table of Contents

Foreword

While it has received practically no attention from denominational leaders, seminary professors, journalists, or demographers, one of the most urgent problems facing Christianity on the North American continent is the product of a severe imbalance in the population. Our culture includes an excessive number of people who enjoy making others feel guilty and too few adults who can laugh at themselves and at their foibles. The most highly visible dimension of this imbalance is the overabundance of adults who gain considerable pleasure out of a huge variety of efforts to make their pastor feel guilty about being less than perfect.

While it is widely assumed, especially among pulpit search committee members, that the Creator intended every ordained minister to be a perfect and faultless human being, slightly over one-half of all pastors do display faults and shortcomings in their personality, gifts, and skills.

This book has been designed to (a) reduce that imbalance in the population and (b) comfort those pastors who are less-than-perfect Christians. That minority of the ordained clergy who are without faults and who do not reveal any imperfections in their character will have great difficulty in comprehending the perspective of the authors. It would be wise for them to read no further. While the Surgeon-General has yet to rule publicly on this matter, the evidence suggests that reading this book could be injurious to the professional health and the personality of those pastors who are without fault, who have never had a parishioner or a denominational official or a seminary professor lay a guilt trip on them, and who find it painful to laugh at themselves. Their purity and innocence should be protected, and that is the purpose of this warning.

This book also can be a useful text for the pastor who is seriously interested in a training program for newly elected officers of that congregation. The five-percent principle will help these new officers understand more clearly the doctrine of original sin as well as why that church seems to move from one financial crisis to another.

This book will help the literalists among the members understand why things are seldom what they appear to be. This is a crucial lesson, not only for pastors and officers, but also for new members. Daring pastors may want to use this book as the text for a new member orientation course.

Perhaps the audience that will benefit most from the wisdom contained in this volume will be the recent seminary graduates who have the opportunity to study it during that journey between departure from the seminary and arrival in that first pastorate.

Thus this book can be the answer to that frequently raised question asked by mothers, fathers, aunts, uncles, former pastors, and beloved professors, "What can I give Terry as a present for graduating from seminary?" The best answer, of course, is a box of accumulated wisdom. Between the covers of this book is a remarkable inventory of wisdom on how to be a happy, loving, forgiving, tolerant, joy-filled, reflective, and even, occasionally, effective pastor. What more could a seminary graduate want?

Another audience for this book is composed of ministers nearing retirement who, as they look back over their years of faithful and devoted service, still are puzzled over why so often things did not turn out as they had anticipated. The book will enable them to reflect on their pilgrimage with insight, laughter, and new satisfactions.

The big audience for this book, however, is composed of Christians, both lay and ordained, who share five characteristics. They believe laughter was a gift that God intended us to use. They are sufficiently mature and they can laugh at themselves. They enjoy mature reflection more than sharing in the search for a scapegoat. They feel a deep love for the worshiping congregation, despite all its shortcomings. They feel a deep and abiding love for all of God's children.

This book has been written for those who share these characteristics, and they will enjoy it.

Lyle E. Schaller
YOKEFELLOW INSTITUTE
Richmond, Indiana
May, 1985

Preface

The Penguin Principles? That will take some explanation! "Pastoral pain" blended with a "unique joy" was the beginning of the whole thing; the joy and pain of a combined total of fifty-two years in the parish ministry!

The authors of the Penguin Principles have served six different parishes stretching from Cuyahoga Falls, Ohio, to Salt Lake City, Utah, to Spokane, Washington. We love the parish and have no regrets about our chosen profession. We have experienced the pain and also the joy common to all ministers who take their work seriously.

We understand the "unreal expectations" laid upon the pastor by people in the church. "We want an interesting preacher, a well-organized administrator, a dynamic leader, a worker in the community, a comforting counselor, a careful scholar, an up-to-date teacher, a capable youth leader, a successful fund-raiser, a zealous missionary, a loving shepherd of the flock, and a fine Christian example." We are also aware of the "try harder, be strong, hurry up, please everyone, be perfect" feelings we put upon *ourselves*. It sometimes feels like climbing a steep mountain with every ounce of energy, but never getting to the top.

If church attendance is low, if the offerings are behind last year's, if the sidewalks aren't cleared of snow, if the flower beds aren't weeded, the fault-finding finger always seemed to point in the same ministerial direction.

Add to that the feeling of the pastor at the subtle criticism that comes from the distorted use of the annual statistical reports; add to that the competition and jealousy of fellow clergy; add to that the "put-downs" of theological professors whose book we haven't read and whose ideas we couldn't understand, and you'll have some idea of what we mean.

If you put all those distorted feelings together, boil them up inside a person for ten to twenty years, there is bound to be an explosion! *For us* it was an explosion of tension-releasing laughter as we sat down and talked of forming an organization of "militant ministers" called The Order of Parish Penguins.

In late night "bull sessions" The Penguin Principles began to fall into place. What are the *realities* of the parish ministry?

What were the *fantasies* about church life that we had brought with us from seminary? Are there ways those realities can be dealt with? Are we really being kind when we bear or even take away other people's responsibilities? Where in all this does Christian love and pastoral concern fit in? Do we really serve God, people, and the church by letting our destructive feelings destroy our effectiveness? How many of those feelings were we putting on ourselves? Is this view of the church and the ministry really Biblical?

We proceeded to test these principles in the "real parish ministry." The Penguin Principles are the results of many failures and a great deal of "slow learning" to determine what actually works in the parish ministry as it is. Through the years the Penguin Principles became the means by which God gave us a new maturity and joy in the ministry.

But why the *Penguin* Principles? The more we studied about penguins and their life in the Antarctic, the more apt the comparison seemed to be.

Penguins seem to have that unique dignity that many people expect of the pastor. Yet, as dignified as penguins seem to be, they look so ridiculous as they waddle around on the ice. Something of that same absurd dignity applies to the pastor's ministry as it really is. The task is so "glorious," but we are so laughable as we blunder through in the work of the kingdom!

Penguins are very sensitive to heat. Their bodies have a special "feather-fluffing" mechanism to release the heat when the temperature is above freezing. Pastors too are very sensitive to "heat" and need a similar mechanism when they are being "roasted."

Penguins have some very treacherous enemies, such as the leopard seal and the killer whale. The ones who live to ripe old age learn to look carefully before they leap. Pastors, too, must continually be aware of the reality that is found in the church, organizations, and people! Only ministers who have learned to walk "circumspectly" live to a ripe old age in their profession!

Penguins are indeed very small and defenseless beings. There is nothing "authoritarian" about a two-and-one-half foot bird that can neither sing nor fly. Their only defense is to wave their flippers and "tweak" you to get your attention. What could be more harmless than a "gaggle of penguins?" So also "militant ministers" are rather small and defenseless. They don't want to hurt anybody. They only want to wave their arms and "tweak" you now and then to get your attention.

Penguins have a homing instinct relying on the position of the sun. They have been known to travel over 400 miles to return to their rookery. On cloudy days they are lost. So also Parish Penguins receive their real direction in life from the "Son" that is above. On their "spiritually cloudy days" they just walk in circles.

No matter what happens to penguins, they keep their heads high. From a worldly point of view there is little for them to be proud of; but from their Creator, they have gained a special dignity of their own that enables them to keep their heads high. So Parish Penguins keep their heads high in the midst of the *reality* of the church. They may have little to be proud of in the eyes of the world, but they have an "alien dignity" that comes from God.

If the Bible can use the "birds of the air" to describe God's daily care of his own; if not even a "sparrow" falls without God's knowing; if the "wings of an eagle" are a picture of the Lord's comforting strength; if God can use "ravens"to take food to one of the prophets: then why not look to the "penguin" for a picture of what ministers can be like in the reality of the church?

In the course of time we have discovered that *we are not alone* in the experience of "pastoral pain." Professional church workers of all kinds understand what we are talking about. Ministers of education, directors of youth, parochial school teachers and even these church workers' families know the frustration, anger, and bitterness that sometimes inhabit the lives of those who work in the reality of the church. Lay leaders in the church too have experienced the pain. In fact, we have discovered that the Penguin Principles apply to anyone who works with people.

There are many others, who, like ourselves, failed to take the doctrine of original sin seriously enough. There are many others who have failed to see that "agape" has some firmness to it. There are many others who have believed that "to love" means to be "Mr. Nice Guy."

Lest there be any misunderstanding, we are *not* saying that the laity, other clergy, denominational officials, or others are singled out as "enemies." We *are* saying that we pastors are often *our own* worst enemies because we fail to deal with the realities of people, organizations, and ourselves!

This set of principles is not to be construed as a "put down" of denominational officials, the laity or organizational forms. *Nor* is it an appeal to the laymen and women of the church to do something to help their pastor. It is a frank, realistic and straightforward appeal to *pastors* to do something to help themselves. Indeed, we believe that anyone who works with people will benefit from these principles!

Remembering the excitement and enthusiasm with which we entered the parish ministry, we know that many *younger* ministers will read this material with mixed emotions. Is the church really that way? Should "methods" like these really be considered? We ask younger church workers to test these principles in their daily experience and compare them carefully to what they read in the Scripture and observe in the reality of the parish.

Above all, the next time you are frustrated, angry, or ready to quit the ministry, be sure to remember the place on the shelf where you put *The Penguin Principles!*

A word of warning about our style!

We have written a portion of each chapter of *The Penguin Principles* in a "tongue-in-cheek" style of humor and overstatement. It is done deliberately to capture your attention and break through a "mind set" that often prevails about ministry and ministers in the church.

These are not unthinking, sarcastic, or cynical words. They are written to compel you to action, to stir your creativity, and to spark your enthusiasm for moving positively toward maturity and a satisfying joy in the reality of serving God's people in the parish ministry.

We have written intentionally to tease you, to shock you, or to "tweak you" if you will, to *look seriously* at what we are saying. The second section of each chapter is designed to deal with the serious questions that may be rising in your mind. In these sections we would like to challenge your view of your ministry from a "dead serious" point of view.

Chapter six is our favorite. It is vital to everything, but it is most meaningful when it is seen from the reality of chapters one through five. God's "tough love" is the strength every pastor needs to draw on. It's the refuge of the penguin.

Read then. Laugh. Disagree. Get angry if you will. But do not disregard the serious intent of *The Penguin Principles.* Whatever happens, we believe it will help you to move on to greater maturity and fulfillment in your ministry!

The Order of Parish Penguins

Dear Friend:

This letter is your invitation to join the newest and most unique of the minority power organizations. The Parish Penguins is a mythical organization of "militant ministers" joined together to throw off the unreal expectations, the undeserved blame, the irritating demands, and unfair treatment placed on us by those who do not understand!

Have you been "dumped" on lately? Have you been left with the frustration, guilt, self-doubt, and the anger of the experience? Then the time has come for you to stop wallowing in all that self-pity, stand straight with dignity, raise your nose in the air, and waddle off into the fray with the Parish Penguin.

To become a member of the Order of Parish Penguins, please send your name and address with a contribution for postage and handling to me, the Grand Tweaker. By return mail you will receive an official membership card entitling you to all the pain, prerogatives, and privileges of the order.

In the meantime commit the enclosed principles to memory, study the stories which illustrate them, and begin NOW to practice them diligently in your daily ministry. These principles, printed in old English letters on a large piece of parchment or done in the finest felt, make a lovely office banner.

With careful study and serious application, you may be able to reach the rank of "super-pastor." A "super-pastor" can dive into a phone booth at any time and emerge thirty seconds later as a two-and-one-half foot penguin, waddling forward, nose in the air, with unconquerable dignity, ready for any and all icy realities!

Friend, the time for whining, self-pity, and complaining is over. The time for action has come. It's time to break free from the self-imposed shackles of guilt, the doormat stance or the "be all" and "do all" hero role.

Too long we have smiled in passivity. Too long we have confused humility with being the patsy. Too long we have thought silence to be a virtue. Too long we have not asked for what we need. Too long we have let our "love" enable others to be irresponsible. *It's time to do things differently! It's time for a change!*

JOIN THE PARISH PENGUINS TODAY!

> *Powerfully Yours,*
> *THE GRAND TWEAKER*

Dedication

To the members and friends of:

Our Savior Lutheran Church, Bingen, Washington
Hope Lutheran Church, Greenacres, Washington
Redeemer Lutheran Church, Spokane, Washington
Christ Lutheran Church, Murray, Utah
Beautiful Savior Lutheran Church, Spokane, Washington
Redeemer Lutheran Church, Cuyahoga Falls, Ohio

You have helped us learn and serve, and we love you for it!

Thanks!

Dave and Paul

1

The Five Percent Principle

Despite the pious things we say, at any given time, less than five percent of any group of people in the church is operating with purely Christian motivation. The other ninety-five percent is asking, "What's in it for me?"

"It's a piece of cake," Pastor Al assured himself as he began his ministry in a small congregation. "I learned my job well at the seminary." "All I have to do," he said, "is explain to the members of the Church what God wants them to do. They will do it, and I can move on to greater responsibilities in the Kingdom."

However, if the temptation to give advice is irresponsible, the ability to ignore it is universal! In a comparatively short time Al felt himself going down hill as if shanghaied on a runaway skateboard. Al left his first parish utterly disillusioned. He had assumed that most of the congregation was operating from Christian motives. However, most of them were asking, "What's in it for me?" The five percent principle was at work.

Pastor Ed had learned the proverb in the seminary about the three different groups of people in a congregation. "One third are workers, one third are shirkers, and one third, jerkers!" Perhaps." thought Ed, "I can make that top third grow to be a half," as he worked and preached with great diligence. But, in the same way that rotten apples affect good apples, he found the tendency was for the one third workers to get smaller, not larger. In the last analysis the largest portion of the congregation was asking, "What's in it for me?" The five percent principle was at work.

Pastor Ben thought he had finally discovered the solution to the financial problem of the parish. "If only," he said, "the members will give five percent of their income to the church (and that's only half the biblical tithe), all our problems will be solved." While almost everyone in the congregation verbally agreed with him, the response to the program was discouraging. After two months of the campaign, Ben felt increasingly frustrated. He forgot a basic premise of life. *Only the fool and his money are soon parted.* The natural tendency of all people is to hold on to money, not to give it away.

The greatest test of the motivation of Christians comes in the way they use *all* their money, not just the portion that goes in the offering plate. Despite the beautiful speeches about "dedication," "tithing" and "personal sacrifice," great numbers of Christian people give only because there is something in it for them. It's the five percent principle at work.

Pastor Gordon was once asked how many active members there were in his church. "One hundred," he replied, "Fifty for me and fifty against me." *Gordon had learned the truth of the saying, "Friends may come and go, but enemies accumulate."* It's the nature of people. Few of them serve God or others from "pure" motives. No one can ever really expect to please more than fifty percent of any group of people for any length of time! Pastor Gordon knew the meaning of the five percent principle.

Martin Luther understood the five percent principle. He once wrote, "The defects of a preacher are soon spied. Let him be endowed with ten virtues and have but one fault, and that one fault will eclipse and darken all his virtues and gifts, so evil is the world in these times." What he didn't understand is that his society was in no way unique. It is still true today! *"He who desires the public's ear must endure the public's mouth."*

Pastor Clarence invited a noted theologian for a week-long study program to increase the spiritual vision of the parishioners. Clarence's hope, of course, was that this brilliant teacher, who had great insight into the truths of God and people, would be able to lift the sights of the members to new levels of spiritual love and devotion. Much to Clarence's chagrin, the theologian spent most of his time promoting his new book. Unfortunately, even theologians are often asking, "What's in it for me?" The five percent principle was at work.

The five percent principle also applies to church college professors, bishops, denominational executives, public relations men and fund raisers. In fact, with this group it sometimes seems that it would be closer to the truth to call it the three-and-one-half percent principle! With this group parish clergy must realize that real spiritual motivation is usually in inverse proportion to the pious appearance of the individual!

Through the years Pastor Earl had received many letters from his denomination's local seminary president. When the school was struggling to get enough students to operate successfully, Earl was told, with great spiritual emphasis, to encourage all his young people to consider the ministry as their life's work. This was

God's will for them! However, by the time Earl managed to convince one of his young men to study for the ministry, the need for students at the seminary was not so great. Now the cry was, "We need the *highest qualified* young people to study for the ministry." Pastor Earl's nice young man flunked out. Unfortunately, it is often the immediate need of a school, rather than the "inner call" of the individual, that determines who shall or shall not become a pastor. Even seminary leaders ask, "What's in it for me?" It was the five percent principle at work.

Pastor Fred had known many ministers in his youth. They were, to him, the picture of piety, dignity, and self-discipline. "Once I am ordained," thought Fred, "I'll be like that too." Much to his great shame, he discovered that after he was ordained he was still the same lazy lout he had always been! "I'll just have *to look like a minister,*" he told himself. Tragically enough, the five percent principle applies also to ministers!

Pastor Henry was given $5,000 by one of his elderly members. The old man wanted to disprove the saying, "You can't take it with you." He asked Henry to put it into his casket at the funeral. The day finally came, and the shrewd pastor put an envelope into the old man's casket. The envelope contained Henry's personal check for the entire amount! Unfortunately, Pastor Henry also succumbed to the five percent principle.

Keep it crystal clear in your mind. It's not just the "bad people" in the world to which the five percent principle applies. It's not just the "bad members of the church," the "bad church leaders," the "bad pastors," who keep asking, "What's in it for me?" It's one hundred percent of the *best* of us who operate from something less than Christian motivation ninety-five percent of the time. Yes, *Christians* who know God's love, who know his mercy, who pray with faith, and who study the scriptures are operating with pure Christian motives less than five percent of the time. That's the reality of the five percent principle.

Frank's pastoral ministry received its third severe setback in less than a year. The evangelism program was a lot of work, but the results were disappointing. The plan for the vacation church school was carefully laid, but somehow attendance just dwindled. His request for money and workers for a downtown program for the aging fell on deaf ears. In his honest moments he knew it was not just the fault of the congregation. His own weakness contributed to these failures. He had such great ideals for himself and the parish that he served, but the higher those kinds of goals, the greater the disappointment. Remembering the five percent principle, it is often true that *the greatest enemy of the "real church" is the "ideal church."*

There isn't a lot a pastor can do about the five percent principle, except to be aware of it! Pastor Richard was proud of himself. He bounded up the stairs into the parsonage and gave his wife a big kiss. He couldn't believe that he could feel so good after such a long congregational meeting! Here and there some genuine words were spoken, but mostly it had been filled with the endless words of people evading responsibility, shifting blame, and looking out for their own interests as they did the business of the church. He knew, however, they were only being normal human beings. He was aware that he had responded in the same way many times in relation to other things in life. How silly people must look in the eyes of God! Remembering the five percent principle he had smiled to himself the whole three hours. He was beginning to learn.

Pastor John was nearing the end of his ministry. Through the years, he too had learned the meaning of the five percent principle. He had been used by many fund raisers in the church. He was blamed for the failure of many new denominational programs. He lived through the intellectual "put downs" of the theologians. He had experienced the members of his own church turning against him as he exhibited some of the lapses of old age. But he knew he had done his best, not as "successfully" as some around him, but *faithfulness* was his aim. He slept well at night. He wasn't bitter. He knew no one "had it in for him." It was simply the five percent principle at work. You see, as Ben Franklin said, *"There are very few old idealists!"*

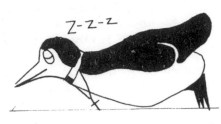

Pastor Ivan introduced a new adult education program in his congregation. He know that there were many members who would respond automatically because they respond to most everything! He also knew the Spirit of God would continue to be at work, to guide, to change hearts and minds. However, while describing the effort that each member would have to put out to make this new program a success, he did not neglect to answer the question the ninety-five percent are always asking. By re-directing and harnessing people's basic self-concern, he used the ninety-five percent aspect to strengthen the five percent principle. In occasional moments of God-given insight, you too can learn to harness the five percent principle to serve God's people. This is our worthy aim.

You might be interested in developing your own "Parish Penguin Stewardship Program!" This program might well contain information to help harness the average person's sense of fair play, responsibility, pride, self-satisfaction, desire to compete, and desire for the influence and respect that comes from being one of the "good members" in the church! Having done your part to manipulate people to raise money, you can be about the *real business* of stewardship, which is the *raising of people who manipulate money for God!*

Understanding the way it is in God's world, it's not the ninety-five percent who ask, "What's in it for me?" that are surprising. It's the five percent who by God's grace manage to rise above their normal desires! It's not the ninety-five percent in each one of us, but the five percent that is motivated to real sacrifice and service that is "God's real surprise!"

Five percent may not seem like a lot, but it's like yeast, like salt. To pay more attention to the five percent principle and

learn to observe the workings of God in people brings renewed hope, confidence, and trust in God's promises! Recognize the five percent for the genuine miracle of the Spirit of Christ that it is!

Pastor Tom found real joy in his ministry. The church attendance was really nothing to brag about. Evangelism, stewardship, and education programs often failed as they did elsewhere, but he found real fulfillment in the small but steady amount of Christ-like love and willingness to sacrifice. He found this in the midst of a growing number of God's people. *Understanding the reality of life as it is, he recognized this tremendous miracle for what it really was! That's the key!*

You may call it "man's natural condition," "original sin," "hubris," or "concupiscence" if you will, but the five percent principle always applies. It has been denied with words, covered up with a show of piety, neglected in philosophy, overlooked by psychology, but it is still a reality.

If you want to escape the utter frustration, guilt, and depression that comes from failing at everything you do, be sure to consider the question the ninety-five percent is asking. You may sound as pious as you choose! Without that mastery, you are a Parish Penguin doomed to drown in the icy waters of self-imposed guilt.

Learn it well! Never let it surprise you! Even about yourself! Commit it to memory. When you are continually aware of its reality, you will have begun to master the five percent principle. Honest appreciation of this principle brings new thanksgiving to God for the miracle that the church truly is! Parish Penguins, never forget it. Your satisfaction and maturity *will* grow!

DESPITE THE PIOUS THINGS WE SAY, AT ANY GIVEN TIME, LESS THAN FIVE PERCENT OF ANY GROUP OF PEOPLE IN THE CHURCH IS OPERATING WITH PURELY CHRISTIAN MOTIVATION. THE OTHER NINETY-FIVE PER-CENT IS ASKING, "WHAT'S IN IT FOR ME?"

Thanks be to God for the five percent!

Items for Reflection/Study/Action

How do you feel about the five percent principle? Is it true? Is the case overstated? Is it too "unreal" to fit the Christians you know? Do you feel this principle is too cynical? Could you say it was right on target? What is *your* observation and experience with this principle in your life? Just where would you place it on the reality scale of zero to one hundred? It might be wise to check out your response with the observation of your spouse!

Does a parish pastor or anyone working with people run the risk of becoming sourly pessimistic by wrestling with the first of the Penguin Principles? Is it true that human nature, even in its regenerated and "re-born" dimension, has the carryover of the "old Adam," and that latent self-centeredness to such an extent that even people who are loved by Christ and love him still are prone to ask, "What's in it for me?" more often than we want to admit? How do you think a parish pastor could make use of the ninety-five percent principle? How can you avoid being a "manipulator" of people? Quickly, jot down your idea in writing! How would *you* do it? How would you feel about trying to put your ideas into practice in the next six months in your ministry? It is the contention of the Penguin Principles that by acknowledging and becoming increasingly aware of the five percent principle, it not only *can* but *should* be done!

Using the five percent principle with honesty, we can *un-manipulate* people, free them and ourselves to be and become, by God's grace, more than we are at this point! *It is the denial of the principle that increases the agony and stifles the maturity God and people desire!*

Is the five percent principle biblical? Can you see a flash of Moses and the people of Israel in the principles? (Exodus 16-35 and Numbers 6-27) Do you hear the Apostle Paul and the Corinthian Christians "going at it" in some of the above situations and illustrations? (1 and 2 Corinthians) How about David, King of Israel, poet, man of God, leader? Do you hear him wrestling with *himself* as he reflected on the kingship, the Absalom incident and the Bathsheba debauchery? (2 Samuel 1-18) Some consider the prophet Isaiah to be among the first of the Parish Penguins because of his "all flesh is as grass" speech in chapter forty. Take the time to check out the message of the prophets. They apparently knew a lot about the five percent principle.

Could it be that even the original disciples of Jesus also gave evidence of the five percent principle at work? Do the disciples in seeking seats of honor and position, by their actions in Gethsemane, and even later at Antioch (Galatians 2) indicate the depth of the pervasiveness of this principle?

Let's ask the questions in a new progression. Is the five percent principle basically biblical? Is it true in our generation? In my church? In my life? How does that make me feel?

In a "success-oriented" world the five percent principle doesn't get much attention. It's painful to consider and, apparently, is mostly avoided both inside and outside the church. To speak of the inclination of a man's heart and will in anything other than progressive, evolving, and improving terms does not get much of an audience — even in the church! However, Parish Penguins have discovered it's the denial of this human reality that is the cause of so much of the hurt, frustration, pain, and disillusionment in the parish ministry and among everyone involved in it!

Both the Holy Scriptures and the daily life of all who make up the Church and the world give us ample reason to be pessimistic about human beings, our inclinations and intentions, but to be everlastingly optimistic about God! To daily re-discover this is to be stepping along toward maturity in ministry. This kind of reality has a freeing power!

By this time some may be asking, "If parish pastors are sometimes really like Pastor Henry (who succumbed to greed for money), or Pastor Fred (with his same undesirable characteristics even after ordination), or the visiting "book-selling" theologian, revealing sin, selfishness, and failure, what will happen to the Church? It will be as it has always been! It will be growing, maturing! It won't happen by cover-up, but by recognition, confession, and God's absolution it will happen! After all, it is our God-given, Christ-transmitted, "alien dignity" that enables a Parish Penguin to truly live. To know and believe this is to be set free to mature in ministry. This is the "joyous skepticism" that comes to a parish pastor whose hope is not built on anything organizational, structural, political, or institutional!

A clear view of what a human being is really like enables Parish Penguins to waddle through life with hearts tilted toward God and wings stretched out to enfold their fellowmen! Even when the ice is slippery!

What is of great importance is the thanksgiving to God for the five percent. For this the trumpets need to sound! For this let the praises ring! For all service and sacrifice that is indeed "of God" ring the bells! It is especially true when others (not you) see glimpses and traces of it in your own life? This is the miracle of God. This is the miracle that creates and sustains the church. This is the miracle that blesses the whole world and even draws a newcomer to the parish ministry! Praise God for the five percent. Yes, even the three and one-half percent!

DESPITE THE PIOUS THINGS WE SAY, AT ANY ONE GIVEN TIME, LESS THAN FIVE PERCENT OF ANY GROUP OF PEOPLE IN THE CHURCH IS OPERATING WITH PURELY CHRISTIAN MOTIVATION. THE OTHER NINETY-FIVE PERCENT IS ASKING, "WHAT'S IN IT FOR ME?"

Thanks be to God for the five percent!

2

The Inverse Insight Principle

Most of the time, in the world of the church, things are not what they appear to be.

Pastor Barbara's head was spinning. Her work was so puzzling! Life in the church is very confusing, especially if you pay attention to what people say!

People had often said, "See you on Sunday." They rarely came. Bright-eyed couples promised before the wedding, "Of course we intend to come to church after we're married." They rarely opened the door. Even faithful members confused her. "My wife and I are planning to make a large contribution to the church soon." Five years later it still had not happened. "I'll be glad to teach Sunday School next year." Next year never came. "I want to sit down one of these days and talk to you about a problem." Contact was never made.

What really had Barbara confused was a visit she made to a drifting member's home. She had called several months before requesting an appointment. They told her they really didn't want her to come. Yesterday, just driving by, Barbara stopped in anyhow! The reception was just the *opposite* of what was expected — very cordial! The visit was lovely! They begged her to come back again! Barbara had discovered one of the "principles of inverse insight."

People don't always say what they mean! If you watch what they do or don't do, you will have a better idea of how they really feel.

Pastor Bill had always felt that the members of his congregation were "humble people." Whenever there was a position of leadership to be filled or anyone was asked to speak in front of a group, most of the people said, "Oh, I could never do anything

like that." However, in the course of time, he discovered that they were anything but shy when it came to criticizing the few who were willing to step out front. *Most of the time when people in the church say "I can't," they really mean "I don't want to."*

It's confusing all right, but it's as common in church as a "wornout hymnal." Words can rarely be taken at face value. Parish Penguins, it calls for inverse insight!

Pastor Jay was filled with increasing bewilderment as a middle-aged couple he admired and enjoyed grew continually more critical of his ministry. He couldn't understand it. They seemed to get more upset, more "touchy" and increasingly angry about so many things — and at so many people in the church too! It seemed they avoided him without cause. Thirteen months later he discovered that the couple's daughter's marriage had gone on the "rocks" and ended in divorce. He could have helped, but they wouldn't let him get close. The pain was too great! *People are not always upset about what they appear to be upset about!*

It's the principle of inverse insight. Most of the time you have to look beyond people's words to know what they really are saying.

It was one of those "sticky situations" that Pastor Frank really hated. The financial recording secretary was behind on her work again. Deposits weren't being made at the bank. The treasurer's checks were overdrawn. There was no accurate way to determine the financial condition of the congregation. Finally, one night it happened. The members of the church council were well into their agenda when the recording secretary entered the room. She took her seat quietly, leaned back with arms folded defiantly, and pressed her lips tightly together. When her turn came she uttered, "No report." When it was time for "new business," she spoke against nearly every motion and also criticized the procedures of the chairman. When finally asked if some help could be provided to assist her, she exploded with anger, resigned her position, and stormed out of the room.

Frank's first reaction was a feeling of "good riddance." But then he remembered something about the home life of his angry friend. The woman's husband, a man of strong faith and courage, had contracted a crippling disease almost ten years before. Members of the congregation visited him regularly and often commented with amazement about his spectacular faith. Meanwhile his wife was left with *all* the work around the house, the care of the invalid, and the work she did for the church. Her smile was very strained as she greeted another group of members who came to pay attention to her husband. There must have been times when her inner fury against the church, the pastor, and even God was ready to explode.

It takes a sense of "inverse insight" to understand. Things in the church are seldom what they seem to be. *There is more to an iceberg than the tip! The poor woman just wasn't mad about what she was mad about!*

What a miracle of God it is, when you find people inside or outside of the church who say what they mean and mean what they say. Knowing how it really is in the hearts of people, the real surprise in the church is that small but precious group of people whose words, actions, and feelings are in tune with one another. To understand their meaning, no inverse insight is necessary.

Parish Penguins, when you find one of those precious people of God, open your flippers wide and welcome them into your embrace. They are almost as rare as a four-leaf clover on an iceberg!

It was a spectacular opportunity for the youth of the congregation. Pastor Richard was excited about the possibilities presented by the congregation's first "bequest." They had been included in an elderly man's will for $5,000. Now the congregation would be able to afford the part-time director of youth they needed so desperately. The youth chairman prepared the appeal well, but at the congregational meeting, one of the "charter members" attacked the program with vehemence. "The money should be used for a lasting monument," he arrogantly proposed, "not thrown down a rat hole by paying the salary for some young kid." The proposal was defeated.

Several months later Pastor Richard was visiting the "charter member" to talk about another subject. The "old timer" looked at the pastor a little sheepishly as he said, "I guess I still carry a lot of clout in the congregation, even though I am getting a little older. Maybe next year we should use that $5,000 for a youth director."

Richard often wanted to write a book about the strange experiences of a minister, but he decided no one would really believe the stories. May God give you the gift of inverse insight, *for in the world of the church, things are seldom what they seem to be.*

Pastor Peter was sent from the seminary directly to a little lumber town in the west. It was his first parish responsibility. His ideals were high, and his motives as pure as the driven snow. However, it was all shattered one night when the chairman of the building committee stood before the congregation and called them all a bunch of "sons-of-bitches" because they wouldn't help him with the new building. It was the beginning of a loud verbal brawl!

Peter, his face pale and drawn, rose to his feet and admonished them all in a nervously high squeaking voice, "Just a minute now, that's not how Christians talk to one another!" The old man who was sitting next to Peter eased him gently back into his seat. "Don't get too excited, Pastor; around here a little fight like that now and then is good entertainment."

It's the principle of inverse insight. *In the world of the church, things are seldom what they appear to be!*

Pastor Norman had just returned from a stewardship conference where he had learned how to raise money in the church. Very carefully he applied the organizational and psychological principles he had learned. He added what appeared to be the proper spiritual verses to the whole program. It seemed to work well.

Its principles were apparently sound. However, it didn't work for long! In the two years following the program, the financial problems of the congregation kept increasing.

Programs using organizational and psychological principles alone are like wearing a girdle. They make things look good for the moment, but when you take the girdle off, the muscles are flabbier still.

Don't be deceived by the appearances of immediate results. Real growth, the kind that comes from the inside, takes a very long time. It's the principle of inverse insight!

Pastor Marvin served a discouraged little parish. Nothing they tried seemed to work out right. At first, Marvin joined the members in complaining about all the people who neglected "hearing the word" and "doing the work of the Kingdom." However, this only made the discouragement greater.

Finally, Marvin decided to try a new tactic. He did his best to show them what God was *already* doing through them. He preached about their potential under God. He noted the ways God was working in them, in their homes, their neighborhoods, on the job, as well as in the church. A new spirit filled the people. Knowing that God indeed was for them, they were eager to do more in his name!

Remembering the opposition and "the way things are" deep in the hearts of men, the truly amazing thing in the church is not the large number of people who are absent and doing nothing, but the smaller number of people, present, serving, and enjoying it!

Things in the church just aren't the way they look on the surface. People know enough about their own failures. It's the good God does *through them* that continues to move them to action!

Pastor Bob urged the people of Holy Trinity Church to get involved with underprivileged children and solo parents in the community; also with a large group of the elderly, and a group of the developmentally disabled living at a half-way house. The people tried. They asked lots of questions of neighborhood leaders. They opened the church building for daily use by the groups. They planned activities and outings, and spent considerable money on publicity, in addition to hours of training and personal contact with the people of the community. After nine and one-half months all three projects were abandoned. It just didn't seem to work. Meanwhile a series of congregational pot-luck suppers were well attended and declared "successful."

In his year-end report to the total church membership, Bob never mentioned the "successful" suppers, but helped the people think "outside the lines" by recalling what they had learned and gained from their contacts with the community leaders and three special groups of people who still had needs. He said, "This is a year to repent of our successes and praise God for what we learned through our failures!"

In God's world sometimes success means failure and failure means success!"

Pastor Bob knew the meaning of the principle of inverse insight. The people were learning it too!

The small town parish served by Pastor Larry was a happy little congregation. The feelings of "community" were good. The people liked one another. "All they need," said the Bishop, "is for someone to lift their sights a little." Therefore he "strongly suggested" some new goals for church attendance, Sunday School enrollment, the mission budget, and new membership. "Now we're really getting somewhere!" said the Bishop on his next visit as he admired the graphs and thermometers he had asked Pastor Larry to post in the narthex. Pastor Larry began to sense what was happening. The Bishop was completely oblivious to the spirit of gloom and discouragement that had begun to pervade the congregation — and Pastor Larry!

Strange as it seems, people are not motivated by higher goals set for them by other people. They are moved to action when they see God doing beautiful things in and through them.

Parish Penguins beware! This is a principle others dearly love to use against the parish clergy. With joy they set high goals for you and your church.

Don't let them kid you, some days just staying in the saddle is winning!

Did you hear the story about the atomic blast which left alive only two ministers and one bishop? After celebrating their first worship service together, the bishop announced that the church attendance goal for the next Sunday was five!

Pastor Otto had been in the ministry seven years, but he was "washed up" already. He had tried to be helpful and kind to everyone, but they had "drained him dry." When the ladies forgot to clean up the kitchen, he felt sorry for them and did it himself. When the janitor neglected to sweep the floor and set up the chairs, Otto did it for him. When people shared a problem with him, he carried it as though it were his own. When his denominational treasurer needed more money, he even donated some of his family's food money set aside for the next month! He did! When the local service club needed more members, he joined. Now everyone else seemed to be doing fine, but Pastor Otto was "washed up." He thought he was being helpful, but, *if you trim yourself to please everyone, you'll soon whittle yourself away!"*

Don't worry about letting others carry their own responsibility. They will be better people for facing their own failures and deciding what they will do about them. *Sometimes it's more helpful not to do the helpful thing.* It's the principle of inverse insight!

The Inverse Insight Principle truly applies to the letters that accompany the documents "calling" a pastor to a new church. It doesn't really matter whether they are written by the interim pastor, the elders, or the chairperson of the congregation. The desire to have a new pastor soon and "shake off the extra work load" usually predominates as the authors of the letters gloss over the failures of the congregation and describe the people in glowing terms. "The mission potential is enormous." "The people are eager to work for God and the church." "This congregation has a magnificent future." "All we need is fresh, new pastoral leadership, and we will be setting new records in the kingdom."

The pastors who receive an invitation like that to a new pastorate had better be able to look beyond those "pride-teasers" and understand the reality behind the "new challenge." They need a special gift of inverse insight.

Pastor Mary discovered a special twist in the confusion that permeates the church. She called it the "filter principle." In all her years of preaching and teaching, she had been trying to make clear the truth that a person was made right with God through faith in Jesus Christ. "Our own deeds, sense of morality and good character are of no value in making a bargain with God. If "salvation" is what people want, they'll have to accept it as a free gift of God." Yet in the congregation she heard the same sentences over and over again, "It really doesn't matter what you believe, as long as you live right!" "I'm not afraid of death, Mary; I've always tried to live a good life." "I've always tried to do my best."

One day as Mary was listening to a sermon being preached by a colleague, she began to analyze her own listening procedure. She noticed how easily she dismissed what she couldn't understand and disregarded the things with which she didn't totally agree. "I guess, like me, people in the church seem only to hear what they want to hear," she said. "It's a sort of *filter principle*. It seems sad, but then again, there's not too much danger that any one of them will be led astray by a preacher, myself or someone else. They only *really hear* the parts of the sermon they agree with anyhow!"

Even God contributes to the confusion that makes inverse insight necessary. Pastor Ken was sick with frustration. He had reached what he considered his "best years" in this surburban parish. It was really "now or never" as far as the real expansion of the congregation was concerned. But, here he was, lying in the hospital, severely injured in an auto accident. His frustration contributed to the pain that throbbed through his body.

After Ken suffered through several weeks of this "double agony," the members of his family began to get through to him with an important message. "While you have been hospitalized, the church has been doing fine. Relax! God's people are rising to the task. In fact, the members are working together so well that things are going better than usual."

Ken's experience in the hospital became one of the most maturing and strengthening events in his life. He was experiencing one of God's great surprises! He discovered that *in God's economy, the hard times are really the "high times" of living!* It's one of the joys of learning the principle of inverse insight! Being aware of it relieves many self-inflicted burdens in the ministry! Learn it well. Commit it to memory. When you are no longer astounded to discover that God's thoughts are not your thoughts and God's ways are not your ways, you will be well prepared for the struggle!

How many times haven't you been dragged "kicking and screaming" through experiences which were God's plan for your growth!

It's all part of the Inverse Insight Principle!

Take a lesson from the penguins. A "slow waddle" through life is fast enough for them. Living on the ice they learn to look carefully before they step. One short, sure step is much better than two fast ones followed by a fall.

So, Parish Penguins, move slowly, watch your step. Look beyond the words people say. Listen to the message behind the message! Think about the ultimate results of "quick successes!" Try to stay in tune with the paradoxical ways of God!

Remember: *MOST OF THE TIME, IN THE WORLD OF THE CHURCH, THINGS ARE NOT WHAT THEY SEEM TO BE!*

Items for Reflection/Study/Action

How do you feel about the Inverse Insight Principle? Is it true? Is it grossly overstated? On the reality scale of zero to one hundred, where do you place this principle? Are things really this mystifying in the church? What is your observation and experience with this principle in your life? In a little while write down some examples. You may be surprised!

Will increasing awareness of this principle cause growth and maturity in ministry? Will it help you personally? How? What are the possibilities? Will it cause you to skid into a negativism that leads to lack of trust and confidence in everyone and everything? Is there a danger in learning the principle "too well?" What might happen? Could an operating awareness of this principle in your daily activity relieve some of the frustration and disappointment that seem to be inherent in the parish ministry? How could you go about mastering the principle of *listening for what people feel and watching what they say?* Young Pastor Barbara, in her home visitation, discovered it by accident and frustration! Can this principle be "taught" or must it be "caught?"

What part does age, life experience, and length of time in a specific church have to do with this principle? Does it enhance or dull it?

Does the Inverse Insight Principle say anything about ministerial priorities and where time and energy is invested? What does this principle say about sharpening our hearing, our active listening? Does the high art of noticing people's expressions, what they're wearing, when and where they appear and/or disappear in the church and community have a bearing on the Inverse Insight Principle?

While reading this next paragraph, please take the time to reflect on the behavior and the words of a member or another pastor who has been avoiding, criticizing, opposing, or in some way "dumping" on you, or others, in the church lately. What has or has not been happening in the home, family, job, or among the friends he/she used to keep? If you don't know, could you find out? Does this have any bearing on the way he or she speaks and acts toward you in church meetings or group activities?

Making a list of the inverse insights you have concerning people you care about and want to serve will often pay a handsome dividend! Maturity in ministry often takes a jump instead of a slide when that happens! It's something this Parish Penguin discovered after sliding into the icy waters more often than he wants to remember!

Is the Inverse Insight Principle biblical? Can you picture, in your mind's eye, Moses and the people of Israel moving slowly through the wilderness of Sinai and northward? Did Moses ever get confused listening to the various and often opposing messages the people gave him? Can you imagine young Joshua, newly appointed leader of Israel, hearing the nation pledge allegiance to him with those startling words, "Just as we obeyed Moses, so will we obey you!" (Joshua 1:17)

Please read Deuteronomy and Joshua again soon! That's the one responsive liturgy Joshua probably regretted for a long time! However, he was forewarned and consequently fore-armed. He too remembered the wilderness. Never forget it!

Can you imagine old Isaac scratching his head, poking his finger into a waxy ear, rubbing his eyes, and stroking his beard in recurring rhythm trying, with all his might, to understand the deception Jacob and Rebekah had just pulled off on him (Genesis 27)? He knew something about the Inverse Insight Principle after that encounter! He probably knew it ahead of time, but couldn't imagine that happening in the house of a Godly man. It was terribly painful. You probably know the feeling!

The Bible often records that Jesus went off by himself for a time of prayer, meditation, and just to "get away." Can you envision the Lord with his head bowed, cupped in his hands, trying to understand the on-again off-again faith and commitment of his disciples? Please think about that after your next, less-than-expected Council meeting!

Perhaps you too know the struggle of Paul trying to understand those two warring parts of himself and every human being in Romans 7. Or perhaps you've been to a church convention where you never could figure out why delegates who voted for one position and policy one day appeared to take a complete turnabout the next day! If you've ever had that experience, you can identify with Paul as he learned the Inverse Insight Principle while endeavoring to comprehend his friend Peter who both *would* and *would not* eat with gentiles. (Galatians 2)

The Inverse Insight Principle causes Parish Penguin Pastors to look at the environment, the setting, the pluses, and the minuses

in the lives of those with whom they serve. It helps us laugh at ourselves and with others too! Being too serious diminishes the possibility of learning the Inverse Insight Principle very rapidly. Many a would-be Parish Penguin Pastor has been lost because of failure to learn this principle soon enough! It's as vital to survival in the parish as a good sense of humor!

There is more!

Theologically, and evidentially, every Christian is still both "flesh" and "spirit," "old Adam" and "New Man," *simul iustus et peccator.* (Romans 5-8 and Galatians 3-5) While we move toward maturity in life with God (Ephesians 4), we do not entirely trust and love the Lord. We let our need for external status, recognition, approval, praise, and "rightness" often get in the way. It affects us and others. Do you recall Pastor Richard's experience with the elderly gentleman who used his status and clout to stop the hiring of a youth director? In reality there are a lot of different "selves" that struggle forth from each person, pastors too, as the struggle of the "old Adam" and the "new you" continues this side of heaven.

Saint Paul, Augustine, Luther (and perhaps, you too) knew it well. It did not impede them once it was truly recognized for what it is. The Inverse Insight Principle helps us remember this theological dimension of ourselves and everyone else. It also causes Parish Penguins to rejoice and give thanks to God for the work of the Gospel and the Spirit in the lives of God's slow-blooming chilren! *Be glad for the growth! Don't curse the lack of it!*

Listening attentively, even when they do the opposite of what they say, a Parish Penguin Pastor can begin to love people enough to let them bear the natural consequence of their own actions and attitudes while not whittling himself away to nothing trying to "correct" them! Do you recall what Pastor Otto did to himself and his congregation when he failed to learn this principle? He was whittled *down* and they never grew *up!*

The Inverse Insight Principle has its greatest value in helping us to remain ever optimistic about God. God is still at work in the folly and confusion that is often characteristic of the institution called the church on earth. Do you recall what God was doing in and through the people while Pastor Ken was hospitalized, all bent out of shape? The Inverse Insight Principle could well deliver us from ourselves and daily reminds us to "lean not unto our own understanding." (Proverbs 3:5)

MOST OF THE TIME, IN THE WORLD OF THE CHURCH, THINGS ARE NOT WHAT THEY SEEM TO BE!

3

The Ecclesiastical Friction Principle

*There is a friction in the church that burns up enor-
mous energy, consumes endless hours, smothers
creativity, impedes progress and often creates quite a
little heat!*

Pastor Paul and his wife had carefully drawn up a plan for
a new deck and patio for the parsonage. They completed an esti-
mate of the cost and even worked out a way this improvement
could be paid for with no increase in the church budget.
"However," they said, "the men of the church know so much
more about these things, we'll let them work it out." The church
leaders delayed, consulted, talked, sketched, haggled; some even
suggested that it might be better to give the pastor a housing al-
lowance and let him provide his own home. Four years after a
series of congregation meetings, a study by an architect, and a two-
year delay because of lack of funds, Paul and his wife still live in
the "deckless" parsonage.

You can count on it; the more people who get their hands
on a good idea in the church, the slower it goes! Committee inefficiency is multiplied by the size of the committee!

"In the Old Testament they would have called it a prophetic
vision," dreamed Pastor Bart as he developed the pieces of his plan
for the establishment of a new mission in the neighboring suburb.
First, they could sell the piece of prime property next to the
church. Encircled by homes already, there was little likelihood
the space would ever be needed for expansion. The money from
that sale could be used to purchase a piece of property in the suburb
and make the down payment on a utility building with adjoining
swimming pool. With good management a nursery school, a public

reception room, and a swimming club could pay the expenses of the operation, while a Sunday School and church could be conducted there on Sunday.

To the members of the council it seemed more like a *"nightmare"* as they tried to wrestle with their sentimental attachment to the piece of property next to the church, their fears of bankruptcy, the effort of it all, and the breaking up of the close fellowship of their parish. Pastor Bart left the council meeting frustrated and bitter, but wiser. A great inspiration had gone up in the smoke of Ecclesiastical Friction that exists in the church. The real issue had to do with introducing change into the life of people in order to meet an opportunity to *be* the church, the servant people of God.

Pastor Quincy discovered the Ecclesiastical Friction Principle can hurt you. He was one of those aggressive personalities with a lot of "drive." He worked hard on creative and progressive programs and expected the people of the church to do the same. Unfortunately, their speed was not his speed. After four years of foot-dragging, in witnessing, evangelism, and caring for the elderly of the community, the people continued to resist the pastor's ideas and instead began to criticize some of Quincy's personal bad habits. He felt misunderstood, deeply disillusioned, and unsure about what had happened. He only intended the best for the people and the church. He left the parish.

When you rub too many new ideas on a congregation, you are usually the one who gets burned. Or to put it another way, parishes are like rubber bands; there is a limit to how far they

can be stretched, and when you go too far, you're the one who gets snapped!

There's the story about a little boy who tried to get a quart of water into a pint jar. The pint jar wasn't a failure because it couldn't hold a quart of water. "One pint" was simply its capacity. Congregations are a little more flexible than glass jars, but not much!

If ever the fiery zeal of the New Testament Church was to be recaptured in a modern-day congregation, Pastor Susan hoped it would be in her little parish.

She preached with an enthusiasm that couldn't be matched in any other pulpit in town. She made monthly visits to nearly every home in the parish to encourage Bible study, prayer, and evangelism. At first the people were excited about their hard-working minister. But when she shouted, "Remember what happened to Ananias and Sapphira" as she urged the people to give more of their earthly goods for the Lord's work, they had enough. At the next meeting of the congregation they side-tracked her enthusiastic program of total stewardship with a long discussion of her failures, especially her neglecting the parsonage lawn. Pastor Susan was badly burned in the friction that existed in her little parish. As a wise old German once said, "He who tries to drain the last drop from the tankard will have the lid smashed down on his nose."

Ecclesiastical Friction doesn't exist just in the congregation. Denominational committees, made up chiefly of ministers, often excel in this energy-consuming process.

Pastor Ed had voted for the establishment of the new Commission for Ministerial Mental Health. He was acutely aware of the kind of pressures he was under and also what was happening to the emotional lives of his brothers and sisters of the cloth. But when he spent another hour and a half filling out a third psychological testing form, he began to wonder if the new Commission was doing more to create emotional problems than to strengthen the emotional health of the clergy! With a "pious curse" he tossed the whole thing into file thirteen.

Sometimes increasing the "helping structure" in the church does more to create problems than solutions.

Jim slumped down in his swivel chair in utter despair. He had just listened to the third "really good idea" for solving the congregation's budget problems. There was nothing wrong with the ideas. Several, in fact, were intelligent and creative. But everyone automatically assumed that the pastor would be the one who would immediately put them into action. And if he didn't succeed, Pastor Jim knew exactly who would bear the blame for the failure of somebody's pet idea. *"Unfortunately," said Jim, "there is no shortage of new ideas in the church, only people who are willing to make good ideas work."*

It's all part of the Ecclesiastical Friction Principle.

"I want to compliment you for all the fine things going on

at St. John's Church," said the District President on the telephone, "You are doing a fine job in what has been a difficult parish." "Yes," thought Pastor Andy to himself, "there has been a lot of activity in the congregation lately." But what really bothered him is that it all centered on what the congregation was doing for itself. The "machine" ran pretty well, but in terms of God's mission, it wasn't really doing very much for the people of the community or the world. A part of the Ecclesiastical Friction Principle is the confusion between "movement" and "motion." "Is St. John's just 'running in place' or is it straining to achieve its 'high calling in Christ,' pondered Andy. "I hope it's not one of those congregations that has aimed at nothing and hit it!" It was Confucius who said, *"whoever keeps his eye on his navel will surely go round in circles!"*

Pastor Igor found the Eccesiastical Friction Principle at work not only in the congregation and denomination, but also in the local Christian community. His neighboring pastor from the little independent church down the street stopped in to see him one morning. After a few words of introduction, he began to describe to Igor the new evangelism mission he was proposing for the community. Though Igor remembered somewhat skeptically that his neighbor never answered any of *his* invitations for cooperation, he was quite taken by his clergy brother's obvious commitment and sincerity. Besides, being negative about evangelism is something like opposing patriotism, prayer, or motherhood! Despite the gnawing feeling inside, he decided to go along with this neighbor's program. "Perhaps this time I am listening to a man with true prophetic vision," he said hopefully. After seventeen planning meetings, forty-seven telephone calls, fourteen evangelism visits, four less than this month last year, *one* elderly lady joined the church.

Late that night as Igor was sitting wearily at the fireplace with his collar loose about his neck, there was a knock at the door. It was the Browns from next door. They had been close friends and good neighbors for over six years. "Igor, we've talked a lot as friends during the past years," they said, "but tonight we need your professional help. Our grandson is ill and in the hospital and is not expected to live. Does God really care?" With a warmth he was never able to generate for a program developed by a self-appointed evangelist, in simple words, he shared the message God wanted these dear friends to hear.

Despite human efforts to impede it, the church seems to plod onward at God's own speed. It pays not to take human efforts too seriously. It's the "shove from above," not the "blow from below" that makes God's church go!

After years of wasting energy struggling with the Ecclesiastical Friction Principle, Pastor Glen finally found an opportunity to use it constructively. One of the members of the congregation heard about a new system of giving Communion that really sends "tingles down your spine." Glen swallowed hard, but thought fast as he referred the matter to a committee in the congregation. "There's no way you can be opposed to a thrilling participation in the Lord's Supper and come up smelling like a rose. When, and if, it ever gets out of committee, it will look so different no one will be able to recognize it. What a magnificent device," he thought to himself; "if only I can snag up all the rest of those well-intentioned but unworkable ideas in committees, we'll at least be free of those "time wasters!"

"Creative pitfalling" is the Parish Penguin term for Pastor Glen's maneuver. It's a useful technique for dealing with any unworkable, low-priority, time-wasting idea that enters the pastor's study. Remember it well. It is usable for side-stepping that difficult visitor, irritating piece of mail, or pesky telephone call. The skill

of "creative pitfalling" has saved many a frustration! Use it sparingly, and wisely!

It was a magnificent idea. The local school for the retarded needs a building badly. The financial resources seemed to be available, but finding land was a problem. Pastor Herman thought about the two vacant lots the congregation owned alongside the church. It would be another century before they could possibly need that space.

"Could it happen that the church could lease the land to the school for the retarded and make arrangements for evening and weekend use of the school? It might even be possible for the church to add a gymnasium for the use of both school and church." It was one of those masterful, genius-like ideas that could benefit everyone.

But Pastor Herman remembered all the other "good ideas" that had been swallowed in the quicksand of church meetings. "Not this time," said Herman, as he began to pray with special devotion and to scheme like a professional quarterback. "Shall I pass, go around the end, or use a power drive up the middle?" He had to decide which natural tendencies to knock down a good idea would need to be blocked out. How could he mix up his plays before the final presentation when he would seek adoption of the "master plan?" "Oh God," he begged, "if it's your will, help this idea to get through."

It was late in the evening when Herman came home from the meeting, but he was as excited as ever! He picked up his son's football and spiked it hard against the back steps as he shouted, "touchdown!" Herman knew now that with God's help a good idea, finely tuned, *can* come through the morass that is often the institutional church!

After years of foot-slogging through the energy-consuming mire of the institutional church, Pastor Hans finally thought he could see it in perspective. He tried to pick and choose carefully those creative ideas that were within the realm of possibility and that would really serve the needs of people in a meaningful way. These projects were worth every ounce of effort and breath of prayer. The rest he let get lost in the inefficiency of the organization. Even with the "good ideas" it was "win a few, lose a few!"

In time, however, Hans came to see how miraculous was every "success" in a church made up of human beings. As his hair silvered, his anger over the lethargy in the institution mellowed, and he came to thank and praise both God and the people he served for the blessed ideas that helped people. *When one faces reality in the church, it's not the failures, but the successes that are so amazing!*

Glimpses of heaven are seen in the plans, ideas and procedures that help people grow, live and mature in life with God each day!

It is miraculous that many good things do happen in spite of the friction! Give thanks to God for every one of those people-helping and God-honoring ideas that blossomed and grew!

Learn it well! Commit it to memory! You can afford to lose the poor ideas in the Ecclesiastical Friction of the Church. Learn to hone your helpful ideas "razor sharp," slicing quickly through the morass that is often characteristic of the church on earth, and you will have made beautiful progress!

"THERE IS A FRICTION IN THE CHURCH THAT BURNS UP ENORMOUS ENERGY, CONSUMES ENDLESS HOURS, SMOTHERS CREATIVITY, IMPEDES PROGRESS AND OFTEN CREATES QUITE A LITTLE HEAT."

Items for Reflection/Study/Action

Do any of those events and stories sound as if they could have happened to you? Do you identify with the evangelistic zeal of Pastor Ralph and the pain that comes from trying to get a pint-sized congregation to hold a quart of good ideas, procedures and practical concerns for others?

On the reality scale of zero to one hundred where do you place this principle? How closely does it fit the reality of your pastoral experience? How does it work out where you live? Is the Ecclesiastical Friction Principle a huge "put down" of God's People? Is it too critical of the way the institutional church functions? Is it a denial of the power of God? Does it sound too anti-organizational to compel serious consideration? Do you think a young pastor can grasp this principle? Would it be better understood by the more seasoned veterans of the ministry? Does this principle have to be "caught" or can it be "taught?" Will awareness of this aspect of the life of the church promote growth and maturity in ministry? What scars or hurts might it eliminate? How? What does it say about the way change is introduced? How could it help you personally?

The Ecclesiastical Friction Principle raises some questions about the humanness of pastors. How would you, or your church council, feel if you deliberately identified some of your past "neglect" of undesirable ideas as "creative pitfalling?" Can you live with that? Is that considered unprofessional, "un-pastor like," immoral, inconsiderate, indecent or dishonest? Would that stir up guilt and anxiety feelings within yourself or the parish?

In the past, what have you done to handle those feelings arising from someone else's time-consuming but non-productive ideas that were foisted on you to fulfill? How will you deal with that reality in the future? Does this principle cause some creative thinking?

Does advance planning and developing of strategy in facing these realities give off vibrations of "manipulation" inside you? How *do you* go about meeting a goal that you are convinced will help many people, but also incur resistance? Do you feel dishonest in considering this principle? Does this minimize the Spirit's direction in life? Where does the Holy Spirit of God enter the Ecclesiastical Friction Principle? Does God continue to work "*all things* together for good?" (Romans 8:28) Could this often-quoted passage become an excuse for sloppy planning on your part or on the part of the parish? Does misinterpretation of that passage promote personal fossilization and loss of creative ideas in ministry? Does the spirit bring the judgment of God upon fearful and "playing-it-safe" disciples? Does the Spirit use the human gifts of organizational principles, procedures, psychology, and the principles of human relationships to benefit the church and the world? Does "praying about it" make an idea right, good, useful, worth seeing through? Do people need spiritual "signs" before they take action on a plan or idea? Is it Biblical to anticipate that some plans and ideas deemed to be "of God" are simply not functional or worth the effort, or perhaps really *not* his will? How do you know in the midst of a church council or congregational meeting?

Is this principle biblical?

Considering the principles previously discussed, what does the Five Percent Principle, people asking, "What's in it for me?" have to do with the friction that often clogs up the ministry of the Church? Does the pastor's feelings about "job security," role position, and status enter the picture at this point? How strongly?

Can you grasp the sight of St. Paul (Acts 22ff) using the Ecclesiastical Friction of the Jerusalem hierarchy and the Roman government to the advancement of the Gospel and his own advantage, when he "appeals to Caesar?" Some may interpret this as the panic of a man about to lose his life, or at least a tactical blunder, but many more see in that event the design of a man of God whose vision for the Church and debt of love for all people led him to get his foot in the door of the most powerful palace in the world. Rome! Was his strategy deliberate? Was he aware of his strengths? His resources? His opposition? Had he "played his cards" with discipline and restraint or was it just a big blow-up that God worked out for good for later generations? Parish Penguins vote for the former!

God called upon Joshua and Caleb to plan a strategy to enter the Promised Land avoiding the delay of Ecclesiastical Friction. (Numbers 13ff) They could have pulled off the plan, but fear, unbelief, cowardliness, and rebellion led to a forty-year postponement of God's good idea! Only two out of the whole congregation lived to see the idea blossom! Talk about the effect of Ecclesiastical Friction! Wow! Have you heard of the same thing happening in some parishes and church organizations today?

Remember that Pastor Bart had a forward-looking, people-serving idea about that mission nursery school, swimming pool, and utility building in the suburbs. Pastor Herman had an equally unique idea about helping the school for the retarded with the ideas of the land for a combination school/gymnasium to benefit both the retarded and the congregation. One man experienced disappointment and the other satisfaction over what happened to the ideas. What factors in dealing with the "friction" that's bound to arise would you be aware of if you had opportunity to plan similar ventures?

What happens to the spirit of a minister whose good ideas are dismissed or simply ground to dust in the mire of organizationalism? Can this be avoided? What's *your* strategy for dealing with the "heat" that good ideas are bound to produce?

The time to tackle the realities of the Ecclesiastical Friction Principle in the parish is *NOW! By God's grace, there is an immeasurable distance between "late" and "too late!"* A few well-chosen and finely honed ideas, kept out of the hands of too many "cooks" or "camel builders" (that's a horse built by a committee!), can unleash a shower of blessings in congregations and communities!

Since God works in and through people with his Word and Spirit, all talents and resources can and must be used to avoid the Ecclesiastical Friction that smothers creativity and impedes the progress of the parish and its priests!

WHAT CAN BE DONE?

Keep your ear attuned to the Word!

Keep your eyes open to the real world of real people.

Look for the hurts, fears and needs to be met with the grace and living power of God.

Measure the ability of your parish.

Preach to the potentialities of God's People.

Prioritize your plans.

Consider the power of the opposition.

Find ways to block out the natural human tendencies of resistance to change.

Clarify and emphasize the benefits to be derived from the plan.

Remember what all of us are asking concerning our own "pay off," while at the same time recognizing that things are not always what they appear to be!

Strategize for accomplishment!

Failure may be the result, so be prepared!

Remember: *GOD CALLS US TO BE FAITHFUL, NOT NECESSARILY SUCCESSFUL.*

Always remember that God's Church *does* move onward at his

pace. The Augsburg Confession says (Article V) "— the Holy Spirit works faith, when and where it pleases him, in those who hear the Gospel." As the Gospel permeates the processes of the Church, God lifts his people. Praise God for the small glimpses of success, the privilege of service, the growth that comes through failure and the chance to help people mature in faith, in love, in hope!

THERE IS A FRICTION IN THE CHURCH THAT BURNS UP ENORMOUS ENERGY, CONSUMES ENDLESS HOURS, SMOTHERS CREATIVITY, IMPEDES PROGRESS AND OFTEN CREATES QUITE A LITTLE HEAT!

4

The Creative Ignorance Principle

In the ministry it is better not to know some things, even if you have to forget them forcefully.

Pastor Tom began his ministry in a small congregation in the country. Since there wasn't much of a program developed, one of his important projects of the week was the layout and print-ing of the bulletin. Some of the ladies offered to help him, but he rather enjoyed this outlet for his creative energies. As the years went by and Tom moved from parish to parish, he developed such office machine skills that no secretary could meet his standards. He felt proud of the weekly production, but inside he knew it had been a "cop out" from many other aspects of ministry. He was trapped by a skill he had learned too well. As Tom grew older, he complained about all the copy work he had to do — but not too loudly!

When you are good at things that aren't too important, it's time for The Creative Ignorance Principle.

Pastor Ulrich was moving to a new congregation. At his first parish he was "Mr. Willing Helper" whenever things needed to be done at church. When the church needed painting, he offered to help. They let him do most of it. When they needed someone to take care of the flower beds, he volunteered. They let him take care of it all alone. When his denomination needed someone to help with fund-raising in his district, Ulrich offered to help. They put him in charge.

As he was driving with his family to his new charge, Ulrich knew it was time for a change. It was like a miracle! He suddenly forgot how to paint. In a flash he developed the strange inability to distinguish a weed from a flower! From that moment on,

when in the presence of denominational officials, he stuttered! He felt the fresh breeze of a "new birth" renewing him! He realized now that he didn't have to know everything and do everything to be a good pastor. The wave of freedom that swept over him was a totally new experience. He had discovered the truth of "The Creative Ignorance Principle!"

Mechanical incompetence is especially valuable for the minister. Pastor Mark had spent his growing years on the farm. There he had learned to repair almost any kind of machinery or build any kind of structure.

That's why his wife could hardly suppress her amazement when she heard Mark saying to some of the church members, "When it comes to doing things with my hands, I'm such a 'klutz.' You people who fix things and build things really have my admiration. If my lawn mower doesn't start on the first pull, I'm in panic."

Once in a while Mark made a secret repair at the parsonage, but for the most part he discovered that his creative ignorance and his admiration of the skills of others paid off in a larger number of willing workers at the church and at the home.

And then there was Pastor Emory! In his woodworking shop he was a veritable artist. He was happy to volunteer to make a new cabinet for the Sunday School office, but before he knew it he had requests for cabinets from the Altar Circle, the Property Committee, the Stewardship Board, and his own irritated wife. While he spent half his time in his shop, the carpenters and cabinet makers in the congregation spent half their

time together criticizing his ministry. When Emory realized what was happening, he felt so angry he could have volunteered to play "Judas" in the "Life of Christ." His woodworking skill could better have been hidden from the congregation and used to please his wife!

When it comes to mechanical incompetence, preachers have something of a head start. No one really expects them to be able to work with their hands. Even St. Matthew (Chapter 25) would understand if pastors who can work with their hands choose to leave that "talent" buried!

The ability to handle money is another "talent" that must be buried deeply. There is nothing more mind-blowing or image-breaking for the average church member than a pastor who can "turn a dollar with a dollar." Unless you want to be classified as a "materialistic minister," a "capitalistic clergyman," or a "profiting prophet," keep that skill carefully hidden. Unless, of course, you intend to give all your capital gains to the church.

Pastor Frank had always considered himself a young man with considerable poise and good taste. But after two P.T.A. invocations and three table prayers at civic luncheons within a week, it was getting a little ridiculous. He turned a deaf ear to his wife's protests as one evening he pulled on his white athletic socks to wear under his black clergy suit. As he stood on stage behind the microphone he "hiked" his pants an extra inch higher as he began his prayer. No one said a word to him about it, but he knew it would be a long time before they called him for an invocation again!

In fact, it worked so well he decided that at the next meeting of the Chamber of Commerce he would read Jesus' words about the "rich man and the eye of the needle." "That little bit of skillful blundering," mused Frank, "should go a long way in reducing the number of my 'invocation invitations.' "

Sometimes, at events such as wedding rehearsals, P.T.A. functions, scout banquets and fund-raising dinners, it is helpful to be just a little "socially inept." When a minister is "too charming" he is always in demand for events of small spiritual significance!

Most of all, don't worry about it, they'll love you anyhow! After all who loves a person who is good at everything? You can always excite sympathy and escape a lot of assignments by saying, "I'm sorry I'm such a dunce!" Being selectively dunce-like is important and very healthy in the long run. Parish Penguins stand tall. You were not called to your profession to know it all or to do it all!

Did you hear about the congregation who told the bishop that their three qualifications for a new minister were:

1. One that doesn't know Greek.
2. One that doesn't sing solos.
3. One that hasn't been to the Holy Land.

The more Pastor Les studied the theology of the church in the New Testament, the more he came to understand that the "ministry" was not *his* alone. He discovered it is, in fact, the privilege and responsibility of *every* believer. The difference between the "layman" and the "ordained minister" was only one of function, not one of responsibility!

It was as if a flash bulb had gone off in his head. "Perhaps the finest personality trait I have brought with me into the ministry," muttered Les in amazement, "is my lazy streak." It all but assures the congregation that while I am pastor, there will be no one to do their ministry *for* them."

Who would have thought it possible? A "lazy pastor," God's greatest gift to the church!

Les had a comfortable smile on his lips as he lay down for his afternoon nap! Later on, after a lot more study, thinking and praying he made a small sign for his office that summarized Ephesians 4. It read, "The pastor is not here to have the people help him do his work. The pastor is here to help the people do their work. Ephesians 4

The pastor is not here to have the people help him do his work .... the pastor is here to help the people do their work.

In the lives of many experienced pastors, creative ignorance has developed into a many-faceted skill. Some have practiced "creative busyness" when asked to perform an "uncomfortable wedding." Others have turned "selectively deaf" when informed of things they would rather not know. So also there may be times to "get sick," to "misunderstand" what you have been told, to come late for a meeting, to rush out of a conference for an "important appointment" or to forget to prepare an assignment! There are even some veterans in the ministry who have developed the mysterious skill of planning funerals weeks in advance to avoid boring and time-wasting events! They can teach young penguins a lot!

There are, of course, those in the church who believe the practice of something like "The Creative Ignorance Principle" is dishonest, double-dealing, slothful, underhanded, deceitful, treacherous and down-right hypocritical. And no Parish Penguins worthy of their icicles would want to be guilty of things like that. *Of course*, it is best to be honest and open about your own limitations. *Of course*, one of the goals of anyone's pastorate is to teach parishioners about *their* ministry in God's church. But while you are working at the endless task of straightening out a faulty image of church and ministry and dealing with the basic, "let the pastor do it," feeling of so many laity, be sure to remember "The Creative Ignorance Principle." Some practice of this form of Parish Penguin reality will always be necessary this side of heaven.

Pastor Victor had a personal secret. When he sat down to share his faith with a stranger, he just couldn't get the words out right. One evening as he sat in the living room of a new family he was visiting, stumbling over his words, the lump in his throat grew so big that it came up and choked him. He could do nothing but confess the truth. "I'm sorry, " he said, "I guess I'm just one of the dumbest disciples around. I can't even share my faith without getting my words all tangled up." This display of humanness touched the new family deeply. Eagerly, they questioned him until they had ferreted out his entire message. *Sometimes it's even best to "witness from weakness."* God has a hand in the principle of "Creative Ignorance." God knows its dangers and blessings quite well!

WARNING! Be careful not to carry The Creative Ignorance Principle too far. Pastor Walter overdid it on Sunday. After announcing the first hymn as "From Iceland's Greasy Mountains," reading the scripture lesson about the "fiery darts of the evil one," and exchanging first letters of the first two words, he proceeded in his sermon to roundly condemn the drinking of "cockballs and hightails!" Walter is pumping gas now!

Learn it well. Commit it to memory. Soon others will stop relying on you to do everything or blaming you for all the faults of the church. How could anyone so ignorant and incompetent be the fault of what is happening in the church today?

"IN THE MINISTRY IT IS BETTER NOT TO KNOW SOME THINGS, EVEN IF YOU HAVE TO FORGET THEM FORCEFULLY."

Items for Reflection/Study/Action

Is there really such a thing as "Creative Ignorance?" Is this not really hypocrisy, the unmitigated deception of the "Old Adam?" Or is it a matter of the "New You" learning how to be "wise as a serpent and gentle as a dove?" Can we benefit from exposing the "tongue-in-cheek" examples that are often more real than we care to admit? Is the church capable of handling this aspect of *real* laity and *real* clergy? Can it be done openly? How would it go over in your parish? Among the pastors you know? What are you now doing that is similar to this principle? What situations come to your mind today? Where would you put the Creative Ignorance Principle on the reality scale of zero to one hundred?

Being creative has often been extolled in classrooms and in pages of books, but real creativity and vitality of ministry in the church are often reduced to ashes by the willingness of pastors to do things to be well liked, but little respected.

Have you met Pastor Tom? He's the printing expert who complained about his busyness, but inwardly knew that *a dose of "creative ignorance" could have changed the course of a ministry that majored in minors.* His people may have wanted him to change, but, come to think of it, maybe not! Pastor Emory, the woodworking, cabinet man, found that his talent created his own cross!

Take a minute. Reflect on the image of the Church and ministry that has accompanied you for many years. What is that image in the minds of the people in your congregation? In your community? How would you describe it? What colors would you use to illustrate it in a picture? If you could sculpture that image, what would it look like? How does that image make you feel when your head is on the pillow and sleep escapes you?

Could you compare that local image with a biblical image of the ministry and the church as the "body of Christ" or the fruit-bearing branches connected to the ever-steady, resource-giving Vine?

What is the ministerial mold that was fitted on you in childhood? Through movies? In the seminary? In your first parish? Does it fit the biblical image where the role of leader is that of servant among servants and where responsibility is shared by all the *laos,* the People of God, without thought of autocratic hierarchy, status, or administrative position? Will this principle help us move in that

direction? Is there a distinction between pastor and people that is unbridgeable in today's church?

Do pastors have to be "perfect" to be pastors in the church? Careful before you blurt out your answer! Think on the *realities* of parish and parsonage life! Answer slowly — after considerable thought!

In your view, is the forgiveness of sin, the acceptance of God through Jesus Christ, more than a doctrine, a creedal statement in the prevailing view of ministry and minister, parish and priest where you live? If it is, the Creative Ignorance Principle can already be "knowingly" laughed about in that place! If not, it may help provide some useful theological discussion of immensely practical value!

Many parish pastors have thought of themselves as having to "be perfect, hurry up, get the job done, try harder, please everyone, be well liked, be strong," — only to find themselves in the "double bind" of also not being accepted for what they are, to be able to change, to grow or to be close to the people they are called to enable for life with God! "Creative Ignorance" has delivered many a "would-be-perfectionist" from becoming a premature "postmortem prize!"

The "cultural religion" of society, divorced from a biblical base, due to rampant biblical illiteracy among official boards of churches and denominations, has produced many church people who want the pastor to conform to their own image of ministry! Add to that the pastor's own lack of biblical insight, and it's no wonder that everyone loses!

How does the "image of the minister" look in your congregation? What "ministerial mold" is commonly fitted to past and present pastors? How does that happen? Is there anything that can be done about it if something needs to be done? Would some "creative ignorance" on the part of the clergy help?

It's a risky consideration! Penguins who have "spoken up" in even the friendliest rookeries have soon found themselves out on thin ice! Pastors who have confessed "the truth" about creative ignorance while at a social gathering of "trusted friends" have sometimes found themselves on similar thin ice at some rather cool

Council meeting only a few months later! Would you agree? Is that too unreal? Ask a veteran Penguin who has slipped on the ice!

Some people are not yet at the point of spiritual maturity, gutsy honesty, or realistic churchmanship where this "truth" about "creative ignorance" can be handled. Some have called it by other names, but few veterans of the pew or the pulpit would deny its existence!

Some among us have chosen to deny its need and in conscientious fashion have faithfully taught all the truths of God's Word and the highest and most holy traditions of the church — but being unable to be human, or to laugh at ourselves — have failed to use the effective method of "creative ignorance," to let others share the responsibilities of ministry. Everybody loses!

An exaggerated "professionalism," expected by some parishes, has kept many a gifted layman from the pulpit and the lectern. On the other hand, the minister who spends a majority of his time week after week with groups, clubs, families, organizations, receptions, committees, fund-raising events, and so on, also produces quite a few vacant pews!

To be or not to be "creatively ignorant," that is the question! How far does one go in learning and living this principle? When? Can it

be performed with a smile? It calls for a clear and continually maturing understanding of the biblical picture of the Church, an awareness of the frailties and foibles of clergy and laity alike and more than a weak grasp on the Lord's hand!

IN THE MINISTRY IT IS BETTER NOT TO KNOW SOME THINGS, EVEN IF YOU HAVE TO FORGET THEM FORCEFULLY!

5

The Tweaking Principle

They'll only do it to you if you let 'em.

This principle lies at the *heart* of the matter! But what does it mean? "They'll only do *what* to you if you let 'em?" Listen for the "pastoral pain" in the following vignettes, and you'll know what the Tweaking Principle is all about.

Coming home from the annual congregational meeting, Pastor Tim blurted, "They did it to me again? Delays, put-offs, not enough money! It's not the right time! We barely made it through last year. You'll have to get along like the rest of us, Pastor! Sorry, we just can't afford to raise your salary this year!"

Tim wasn't blind. He had seen the new homes, the new cars, the boats and campers that were part of the life of the church members. Yet, he was somehow always silenced by the sincere sounding "poverty-talk" that preceded the annual meeting. "I wanted to speak up," Tim moaned when he got home, "but it just didn't seem like the right time."

His wife cringed as her face reddened. She couldn't bring herself to say it, but these people were "using" her husband just because he was a dedicated, consecrated "nice guy." The worst part was, *they only did it to him because he let 'em!*

Pastor Ernie spent thirty-one years of his ministry on the same urban parish. He was from the "old school" as they said. He never asked for much of anything. He didn't even attend the budget meetings. He bought most of the supplies and repairs for the manse out of his already-low salary. "I didn't want to make a fuss or cause any trouble," he'd say to his fellow pastors. Over the years he'd started walking back to the church to turn off the light in the restroom. After all, he lived "just a hop, skip, and jump away," and utility costs were increasing. When the ladies ran out of soap for the dishes after their meeting he'd run home and get some. The custodian often forgot to change the burned out bulbs over the basement stairs, so he did that too. As the years progressed, he felt very much needed — but the growing disillusionment over how he was *really* being treated was leaving an acrid taste in his soul. *He'd let 'em do it to him and they did!*

Being a nice guy is good for your ego, but it usually leads to the "kindness-bitterness syndrome." You begin by being nice and kind, expecting appreciation and imitation, but when there is little response but criticism, you tend to get bitter. Maybe you've only yourself to blame. *After all: "THEY'LL ONLY DO IT TO YOU IF YOU LET 'EM!"*

All of these may seem like little events in the life of a parish pastor, but like a marriage, a pastor's relationship with a particular parish *seldom dies of a massive coronary, it more often bleeds to death from countless small wounds.*

People from the "superstructure" of the church can do it to you too!

"Something wrong at St. Mattews, Don?" queried the denomination exec at the area pastors' conference. He was referring to the slippage in statistics and contributions in the six-month report to headquarters. Pastor Don felt like inviting the man out for a lunch of sauerkraut, maple syrup and jelly beans! Instead, he just took it! He mumbled something about unemployment and the few good contributors who had died, but walking away he felt terribly guilty. Maybe he shouldn't have two nights a week with wife and kids. After all, he wanted to be successful, to do well, to gain respect among his peers, but the resentment welled up like a storm deep inside. His eyes hardened as dislike for the "institution" continued its ugly growth. The tragedy was, *they only did it to him because he let 'em.*

Those many little things that happen to the pastor can really "kill a ministry."

Whenever she reported to the church council on her activities, Pastor Alice whitened as if overcome by bleach. Some council members were convinced she was a weak pastor, "not aggressive enough for the business of leading a church." Her anxious heart told her the reports were received with not much more than sympathy. Those painful feelings multiplied as council members implied she was not making enough calls on the members or visitors. She let the blame for lack of membership and financial growth rest on her shoulders. The "try harder, hurry up, be perfect, please me" message was tightening as the "noose of demand" settled in on her. The suppressed desire for friendship, encouragement, and understanding turned to depressive loneliness. Never confronting the lack of support and serving partnership, she doubted her fitness for the ministry and her usefulness to God.

Today Alice is out of the pastoral ministry, seldom going to church, heavy-hearted, guilt-covered and obviously hostile. But the real truth is, *they only did it to her because she let 'em.*

It's helpful at this point to identify the "buckets of blame" syndrome. In any parish where things are not going exactly right, it is as if "buckets of blame" are being filled and placed in every

opened door, every high window ledge, and every balcony railing. Woe to the careless creature who steps beneath one of those buckets at the wrong time. In a congregation with problems it's necessary to walk circumspectly, covering your tracks with care. With practice you can master the "Parish Penguin Two Step" and avoid the "buckets of blame"!

"If Jesus Christ himself were the pastor, he wouldn't be able to meet the expectations of this congregation," screamed Pastor Carl as he came home from another late night meeting. "Besides being an 'interesting preacher' who always holds their attention, they want a 'dynamic leader' who can bring about changes without irritating anyone; an 'up-to-date teacher' who uses all the latest techniques, an effective 'fund raiser' who gets people to give money to the church with subtle but painless techniques, a 'missionary' who spends most of his time 'pushing doorbells,' a 'charismatic youth leader' who will succeed with young people where parents have failed, and with all that, a 'personal friend' of everyone who always has time to visit. It's like trying to stop Niagara Falls single-handedly, and I feel like I'm about to drown in it all." Pastor Carl couldn't take much more, but the sad thing is *it only happened to him because he let it!*

But what could Carl have done? Or Alice, Ernie, Tim or Don? Is there anything they could have done to have prevented these terrible events? Could they have escaped those horrible feelings? Is there anything preachers can do to prevent things like that from happening in the future? *You can bet your fine-feathered flippers there is!*

Pastor Ted was met at 2 p.m. by the recruitment and development man from the regional denominational college. They exchanged handshakes and pleasantries and closed the office door behind them. The development man got to the point . . . money and students for the college . . . in that order. Something about the "Lord's work" slipped in occasionally. This was the sixth new "developer" to call on Pastor Ted in the last eleven and one-half years. The script hardly changed, and it was as 'irritating as an unreachable itch." He was always being asked to put "the financial bite" on his people. Ted couldn't take it anymore. He began to give vent to his feelings. "I feel like a buck private in the army of the Lord, and when someone in headquarters wants some results, *the buck stops here.* I feel as if I've been invited to be part of this chain of command so that when the chain breaks you can point to me as the weakest link. I feel like a set of false teeth in the mouth of someone who wants another pound of flesh from my people." After the development man recovered from the shock, he realized he was late for another appointment and left abruptly. Ted knew there would always be more fund raisers visiting his office, but he felt clean, so clean inside. He told one of the "powers that be" how he really felt about being "used."

If you want others to stop doing it to you, *tell them how you feel.* Sometimes it even pays to share your anger and show them

what a piece of "ministerial madness" looks like.

Short as he is, the penguin stands straight with dignity. A courageous way pastors can stop others from treating them unfairly is to stand tall with dignity and *"ask for what they want."*

At budget time someone in the congregation can always be counted on to say, "That's an awful lot of money for a person who gets a free house, free car and only works a couple of hours on Sunday"! After a few years of this "repeating scenario," Pastor Steve finally spoke up. He realized that his new stance wouldn't fit the common image of the quiet, meek and long-suffering minister. But if professional people can't go on strike for the kind of working conditions they need, at least they must have an opportunity to use the powers of persuasion. He laid out his qualifications, years of schooling, parallel professional skills and spelled out his work load and his responsibilities and demands placed on him in the last year. He listed his family needs and personal concerns and challenged the people of the congregation to consider a specific salary request. *It was a risk!* He had to show a side of himself that to some didn't look very "ministerial." Steve was well aware that if he would ask for what he wanted from *them,* the parishioners would begin to ask for what he wanted from *him.* But in the long run that could be healthy. Besides, anything was better than the feeling of being used.

Although the congregation didn't give him exactly the raise he requested, it was nevertheless a respectable increase. *Steve had discovered that while you may not be able to solve every problem in the church, you can always improve the situation! They tried to do it to him. He asked for what he wanted and they didn't do it!*

When things are going badly and the verbal "flack" is exploding on every side, pastors often suspect a conspiracy somewhere among the members of the parish, the leaders of the denomination or the members of his community.

Pastoral paranoia never pays! When all is said and done, few preachers are significant enough in anyone's mind to be worth such concerted effort! What makes any pastor believe his or her personal faults are so outstanding? It is simply the "Five Percent Principle" following its normal course in the lives of people. When penguins narrowly miss being swallowed whole by a leopard seal, they know it's not part of a giant conspiracy, just the way life happens to be!

Pastor Gene had a rather offensive posture toward all visiting "finance men from headquarters." This "reality picture" is not recommended in raw form, but used with compassion it's worth noting! He learned to take the initiative in those fundraising visits. He asked "curiously" how the other parishes of the area were doing. As his courage increased, he learned to ask specific questions about the parish to which his visitor belonged. He knew God did not expect him or his church to do everything! He always asked how well others were performing their assignments *before* they asked about what he was doing. He believed in the principle of "a good offense is the best defense" and "the firstest with the mostest"! *After all, they'll only do it to you if you let 'em.*

From the Parish Penguin perspective, telling them how you feel, asking for what you want, and the more highly sophisticated techniques of Pastor Gene are known as "creative tweaking." It doesn't solve *all* your problems, but when aimed sharply at unreal expectations, unjust treatment, irritating demands and undeserved blame, it is a valuable skill!

Parish Penguin Pastor Abraham had lost his wife and now lived in a small community with his son. He was the associate pastor of a large congregation there. However, after a few years the tension between the two pastors had become so serious that they had to put the whole matter to a vote of the congregation. Pastor Abe lost the vote but won the war as he preached his farewell sermon on the basis of the text from Genesis 22:5. "Abide ye here with the ass; while I and the lad go yonder." You see, *they'll only do it to you if you let 'em!*

Pastor Abe has been awarded the "Thirty-Second Degree Grand Tweaker Award." Unfortunately, it had to be awarded to him in the hospital where he was being treated for bruises caused by the stones thrown by his associate. As pointed out before, *tweaking has its risks.* However, it should be noted that Abe laughed so hard from his hospital bed that he was unable to complete his acceptance speech!

At the heart of keeping people from "doing it to you" is learning to *let others bear their own responsibility.* For a good deal of what people "do to you" is the result of a shifted sense of responsibility. Sometimes pastors assume the congregation's responsibilities.

Pastor Tim and his wife were forced to bear the burden of a congregation that was unwilling to fulfill its financial responsibilities. Pastor Ernie accepted the responsibility as "caretaker" of the church. A "statistically motivated" executive laid a burden of guilt on Pastor Don, instead of bearing the responsibility of his own method. Pastor Alice let the people think of her as the "leader" of the parish so they could let her bear the burden of their own failures. Worst of all, she accepted the burden. Instead of letting people learn from reality that their expectations of their pastor were too high, Carl accepted their "impossible dreams" for him and let them drown him in unrealistic demands.

So, Parish Penguins, put aside all your "I-hope-they-like-me" feelings and let people bear their own responsibility. Build a mental wall between your duties and their duties; between what is the result of your failures and what is the result of their failures; between your faulty ideas and their faulty ideas; between the pain you suffer for your own sins and the pain they want you to suffer for their sins.

As with "creative tweaking" a clear definition of responsibility has its risks. If people are called upon to bear *their* own responsibility, they will call upon you to bear *your* responsibility. There will be times for pastoral confession, for pastoral admission of fallibility, for failure and the natural consequences of failure. However, accepting the results of what you "do to yourself" is easier than discovering that "they only did it to you because you let 'em."

Take a look at how God treats all of us. God doesn't take the blame for our sin. God lets *us* suffer the natural results of our own stupidity. God is not just a "nice guy." God is not a coddler. God does not "baby us." God doesn't do everythihg for us or pick up after us like a valet. God deals with us where and as we are.

God even lets the natural consequences, the inevitables, be used to show the outcome of our arrogance and independence. God does not always come running to the rescue like a puppet on our string. God does not shield us from every "blast," nor excuse us when we stubbornly refuse God's invitation and direction. God doesn't make up excuses for us. God doesn't worry himself sick about us, but lets us "sweat it" through our own self-imposed troubles. *God's love is not like a sweet castle made of "gingerbread": but like a skyscraper, it has a skeleton of steel.*

Pastor Jerry was one of the most aggressive pastors that St. James Church ever had. He grew up in an orphanage and had little sense of "roots." He had been compelled to look out for himself almost from the beginning. It was fitting that one of the more biblically literate members called him Pastor Jeremiah. He was a bold spokesman, reliant on God, unafraid of men. He asked clearly for *what God wanted!* He made clear *his own desires* too. When things weren't going well, he told his members *how he felt.* Oh, the people of St. James were no different from other

parishioners, but Jerry knew that *criticism, like poison, only hurts when you take it!* As the years went by, Jerry had his "enemies," but he learned the meaning of the old proverb, *"men of sense learn more from their enemies than from their friends."*

Some of the business and administrative types in the parish were threatened by his manner — but they seldom had any just cause for complaint about his pastoral leadership.

You see, it's better to have a lion at the head of an army of sheep than a sheep at the head of an army of lions. Even being a sheep in a lion's clothing helps. *Or being in the backseat isn't bad if you want to be taken for a ride; but it's most difficult to steer from there!*

Parish Penguins arise! *A TWEAK IN TIME SAVES NINE!* Carve it into your office wall. It's time to stop playing "victim." Remember this principle like your own name.

Be strong, despite the resistance. After all, even a mighty oak was once only a nut that held his ground!

THEY'LL ONLY DO IT TO YOU IF YOU LET 'EM.

Items for Reflection/Study/Action

THEY'LL ONLY DO IT TO YOU IF YOU LET 'EM

Now, what do you think of that? How valid is this principle? Do the illustrations square with your pastoral experiences and feelings? On a scale of zero to one hundred where do you place this principle? Why? Where would you have placed it a few years ago? What, if anything, caused the change? Did you laugh at all the vignettes? Cry? Did you see yourself in more than one? What examples can you add?

Is it possible for a parish pastor to be assertive, yet not crude? Aggressive, but not insensitive? Angry, Yet not mad? Demanding, but not dictatorial? Forthright, yet not offensive? Would the sensitive enacting of this principle bring a new breath of "fresh air" into the churches? What would be the risks? What benefits would be derived? What kind of atmosphere would result? Is it worth the effort on your part?

"Tell 'em how you feel," so that you can be real is a part of the Tweaking Principle. Is that possible in the church today? Who do you tell? The president of the congregation? The Elders, Deacons, Council? The leaders of the Women's Group? The choir? When? Under what conditions? What could happen in such groups if you'd "tell 'em how you feel?" Be careful of your response! Make it responsible! Sometimes pastors tell the wrong people, at the wrong times, in the wrong places and/or in the wrong ways only to discover "the message" coming back like a giant-sized boomerang! More than one penguin has slipped on that icy trail and suffered something like "frost-bit-butt" because of it! Choosing the right persons, at the right times, in the right places and saying how you feel in the right ways calls for strategic planning, acute observations, self-control and disciplined use of the tongue, but the benefits are enduring and accruing to everyone. When Pastor Steve risked telling the right people at the right time about his salary, family and personal needs, he found responsible action resulting. Had he not spoken up, the acid in his soul would have eaten out his heart — and the congregations's too. Responsibility and accountability go hand in hand.

Keeping responsibility where it belongs is a commonly accepted-principle of good organization and business. How do you do that in a church, in a "voluntary" organization where ego needs are often prime motivators? Frustration on the part of both pastor and parish often results from inadequate division of responsibility and low levels of accountability. The clarity in most "Call Documents" is woefully lacking. Vague and general terms are often used. The underlying assumption seems to be that everyone knows what "the Lord's work" is all about in their specific place! "Job descriptions" or guidelines for church officers and boards, as well as pastors, are frequently outdated or nonexistent. As a result, confusion and exaggerated expectation often lead to unspoken pressures, behind-the-back comments, mysterious phone calls, and even unconscious passive-aggressive behavior. Everyone loses!

There is an additional truth in all of this. Pastors who try to keep the lines of responsibility and accountability clearly established can expect to get many assertive responses from the members. That's as it should be! Everyone will win! "They'll only do it to you if you let 'em" works in more than one direction! Agree?

Is there a time and place for pastoral confession?

Confessing failure is often not easy for a cleric. People often do not like to hear it — or even permit it. It tarnishes images! The classic example in the Bible is the fact that Peter's denial of the Lord is one of the few things recorded in all four Gospel accounts! He must have been known not only for his denial, but for his confession and being the recipient of absolution! Others took courage from it. We still do today!

In the parish the pastoral failure to admit mistakes, errors, neglects, sins, and weakness helps create "the Preacher's-on-a pedestal" concept. It's difficult to climb down from there. It's even harder to live in such a "pressurized" atmosphere and position. But never forget, there *will be* some who will delight in knocking the props out from under you! "They'll only do it to you if you let 'em!" Confession is not only good for the soul of the laity, but the clergy too! Do you agree? Besides, it's also the layman's function to absolve in the Name of the Lord! If you let 'em, they'll do it!

Is it *right* to ask for what you need?

Asking for what you need combined with open confession of mistakes, failures and frailties clears the air for real maturity and growth in the church. It's what "practicing the forgiveness of sins" is all about! It's the heart of the faith for daily life. But it's risky! Can you think of a time when this aspect of the principle could have been practiced in your congregation? Your ministry? What might have happened? Would the long-haul effect have been different? How? Asking for what you need calls for an assertive posture that often runs counter to the popular image of the clergy! The image of the "humble man of God" has often been a milk-toast, bumbling, spineless incompetent! To suddenly start asking for what you need and show genuine, healthy "self-love" often creates considerable resistance among church members. It's hard to reconcile this vital approach with "the pastor is here to serve us" image of many. You perhaps remember the story of the deacon who prayed that God would give his needy congregation a new pastor "of poor and humble spirit." What he meant was, "God, you keep him humble and we'll keep him poor!"

The image of the pastor as the humble, long-suffering servant is subject to interpretation by every member of the parish, community and media. It is difficult to re-shape that distortion of the biblical concept, but we submit that it is urgent for the church of today and that the essential message contained in this revered principle is the key to growth in ministry for the total church in every generation. "They'll only do it to you if you let 'em."

Is this principle biblical?

John, chapter six, tells how a newly formed, aggressive group of well-fed men and women tried to "use" our Lord. He didn't let 'em. He counted himself *out!* He would not permit his responsibilities or his gifts from the Father to be distorted to the destruction of the people he loved.

The prophet Amos told a startled Amaziah how he felt, what God wanted him to hear, and Amaziah, for all his governmental and religious authority, "didn't do it to him." (Amos 7) The forthright, honest methods of Jesus in leading his disciples to greater maturity are the highest forms of "servant ministry." They helped everyone mature. He confronted the "sons of Thunder" with their position-seeking tendencies. (Mark 10) He let Peter bear the consequences and responsibilities of his denial, but loved him still. (Luke 22) He spoke very strong words to the Pharisees (Matthew 23) and yet invited a taxman to be one of the trainees for ministry and book writing. (Matthew 9) Later Jesus picked one of the most capable Pharisees, turned his "righteous" life around by telling him how he felt and what he wanted, and gave the world an Apostle who outshone all the rest! (Acts 9 & 22) Jesus, like his Creator-Father, told people how he felt (John 6-9), asked people for what he needed (John 4, Mathew 21, etc), and took full responsibility for his actions (John 10), even to the point of giving his life! "They'll only do it to you if you let 'em" was more than a catchy phrase for the Chief Shepherd and Bishop of our souls (1 Peter 2); it was his way of living ministry!

Maturity in ministry is an on-going process (Ephesians 4) that has roots deep in this principle. They'll only do it to you if you let 'em. How can challenging the unreasonable expectations help you and your parish grow? How can a parish pastor express those suppressed needs in a responsible manner? Could you begin to state more clearly how you feel about your ministry with God's people? What words will you use? Jot them down!

Is pastoral paranoia a growth inhibitor for you? Is there any reality to it? How can you be sure? What will you do about it? When?

With a "belly full" of frustration, unexpressed needs, unresolved responsibility areas, and unadmitted weaknesses and failures, Pastor Carl felt overwhelmed and ready to quit. However, the final outcome was different! Like a baby penguin, he learned from the "Emperor Penguin!" He soon avoided the slippery spots, insisted

on shared and well-defined responsibilities, straightened the lines of accountability, admitted his weaknesses to people who could help, expressed his feelings responsibly, and found a congregation ready to help him get what he needed! Does that sound unreal? We contend that it *can* happen! Not without risk and some pain, but it *can* happen! Maturity in ministry will take place, and the biblical concept of the Church functioning as "the body of Christ" *will* be more nearly achieved.

How will you make this growth happen where you're at? What are you doing now? What do you really want to happen? How do you feel about it? Are you willing to take on the responsibility for *your* words and actions, enabling others to do the same for theirs? Sketch out your plan. Pray for God's guidance. When will you start?

THEY'LL ONLY DO IT TO YOU IF YOU LET 'EM.

6

The Pastor Principle

The ultimate principle for pastors is a "tough love" that looks beyond the irritation of the moment and in the strength of Christ loves people as they are.

The task of a shepherd isn't really as romantic and beautiful as it's often pictured. Together with his sheep, he must face all the hard, raw elements of life. What's worse, sheep aren't really the tender, lovable creatures pictured in the Sunday School leaflets. Not only do they go astray, as the Bible reminds us, but they are smelly, cantankerous, stubborn, and the source of loud complaints when food and water are not to their liking. In northern climates they even time the birth of their young in the middle of winter, requiring a frigid rescue effort to save the life of a lamb. To be a shepherd worthy of his "staff" requires a kind of "tough love" that looks beyond the irritation of the moment and loves those sheep as they are.

The word "pastor" means "shepherd." The pastor's ultimate resource in dealing with people inside or outside the flock is a *"tough love" that looks beyond the irritations of the moment and in the strength of Christ loves people as they are.*

Pastor Joyce was angry as she prepared her sermon. She had received word that ugly rumors about her ministry were being circulated again. "It's time for another barn-burning sermon on "judge not that you be not judged," she grunted as her theology and her anger intermingled!

The fire of her anger cooled suddenly as ten minutes before the service one of the "known gossips" of the parish asked for her prayers for his child whom he revealed was terminally ill. Pastor Joyce's sermon changed its tone and its theology, as it emphasized the second half of the text instead of the first. "To judge others" she noted with sadness "is one of our human sins and frailties, but the ability to escape a similar judgment by God, through faith in Jesus and the forgiveness of sins, is the real message of the Kingdom of God."

Despite her feelings, Joyce learned "tough love" for her people. Overcoming her irritation with the flock, she loved them as they were and fed them with gospel-food they needed most!

Pastor Lou began to develop the sensitivity of an x-ray machine to the half-truths and accusations that came from some of the parishioners, and community organization members too. By one particular couple he had been severely used and abused . . . labeled as a spiritual rubber stamp! Yet with "tough love" he persisted in calling on them, listening, planting the incubating Word, showing them God's better way. He loved this couple. He looked beyond their words and heard the grinding of their fractured hearts. He focused on their actions, not their declarations. It took much longer than he had imagined, but in time the self-deception was confessed, the agony revealed, the gush of tears released, and the calming, binding love of the accepting Father was applied.

In that church "pastor" was not a title but the first name of a friend. In him patience was not a sign of weakness but of concentrated strength. *"Tough love" puts aside hostile feelings and listens patiently for the sounds of pain, fear and loneliness.*

The voice on the phone sounded urgent as Pastor Wayne was called to the hospital. The infant son of one of the young couples of the parish was struggling for life.

Wayne wrestled with his feelings as he drove to the hospital. He remembered well all the promises the young couple had made to him before the wedding about their religious intentions.

But in the joy of newly married love, the promises were quickly forgotten. Worse yet, when asked about their absence, the "pastor's poor sermons" were their excuse. But what ground even more deeply into his soul was the fact the grandfather of the baby was his super-critic in church affairs. His leadership and dominance of the congregation were challenged by Pastor Wayne. He seemed to oppose everything the young pastor tried to do.

However, facing the tears and drawn faces of parents and grandparents, changed the feelings of Wayne's heart. Behind their hostility and weak excuses were people of God who were suffering, and in the other room there lay an infant struggling for life.

"Tough love" is the Parish Penguin description of the feeling and Spirit-given understanding that motivated Wayne to keep coming back to the hospital to spend hours with this family in prayer and "waiting on the Lord." When the infant breathed his last, Wayne cried with his critics.

After the graveside service was over and all condolences were made, Wayne knew that the child had not lived and died in vain. Through him Wayne knew he had learned the virtue of "tough love!" God's kind!

"It's too silly to share with any of the other pastors," thought Augie to himself. "They'll think I've let my imagination run away with my theology again!" Whenever Pastor Augie was irritated with people, inside his parish or out, he looked at them carefully and tried to picture them lying in a *casket* as he officiated at their funeral. It gave him a special perspective on humanity and our individual frailties. Pastor Augie even used his "casket technique" on salesmen who bothered him. Even the bishop himself, when irritated with "his eminence!" Not that he was any more sympathetic with what he considered people's "crazy ideas," but when they talked to him they knew they had a friend. *To look behind the mask of humanity and see the stamp of the "image of God" is the skill of tough love.*

That "tough love" is what Parish Penguins call "The Pastor Principle," the "ultimate strength" in the ministry. *"Tough love" breaks down the shell, crumbles the knees, silences the mouth, "gentles the spirit." It does what no weapon known to man has ever done . . . makes your enemy your friend!*

Is "The Pastor Principle" of "tough love" a *softening* of the Tweaking Principle laid down in the previous chapters?

EMPHATICALLY, NO!

The principles in the Parish Penguin ministry are as closely linked together as the icebergs in McMurdo Sound in the middle of winter. "The Five Percent Principle," "The Inverse Insight Principle," "The Ecclesiastical Friction Principle," "The Creative Ignorance Principle," and "The Tweaking Principle" all talk about *reality*. Without insight into that *reality*, a pastor may be led to believe that loving people in the church is "effortlessly simple." The strategies for dealing with that reality *do something* about the *feelings* that surge up within the pastor as he/she works in the church. All the talk of love one can imagine will not send any compassion through arteries clogged with bitterness, frustration, anger or resentment. FACE THE REALITY OF THE PARISH MINISTRY. PLAN YOUR STRATEGIES WITH CARE. PRACTICE TOUGH LOVE FOR GOD'S PEOPLE.

This is the triumphant shout of the Parish Penguin movement. All together they make up the ingredients of *"maturity in ministry."* All the other principles of the Parish Penguins can be learned by hard work and persistence, but the "Pastor Principle," the ability to show "tough love" is a gift from God alone. God is the Chief Pastor, the master of "tough love." God is not side-tracked by sentiment, by a distorted or twisted "love" that is naive about human hearts and lives. God does not coddle or excuse, but forgives, accepts and blesses. God lets people endure the natural consequences of sin, willful pride and stubbornness, but still continues to practice that life-renewing "tough love" — a love that has depth, fiber and resiliance. *God's* own love! It's demonstrated in Christ, our Lord! It's what God gives to you!

"I call it the Liturgy of Remembrance," explained Pastor George to his wife. "When I begin to find people hard to love, I take off a few hours and page back through my diaries of years gone by."

"There I'm reminded of my inner turmoil as I tried to decide whether or not to continue to study for the ministry. I remember the fear and shame when, once I had decided to become a pastor, I almost flunked out of the seminary. I recall thoughts of suicide as I endured serious doubts about the Christian faith. In my diaries I re-read my reactions to an auto crash that almost took my life, college pranks I was involved in that really hurt people, a potential marriage disaster saved by a broken engagement, my readiness in the first years of the parish to quit the ministry and go home. *What a tough and enduring thing is the love of God, if it could stay with me through all of that."*

"When I remember that," sighed George, "I find it easier to love people just as they are."

Pastor Ike had reached the "confidence stage" in his ministerial life. He had a good wife, two fine children, and had been a parish pastor long enough to "know the ropes." Though he had achieved all the earthly goals he had set for himself, he was aware of a persistent feeling of loneliness and boredom. All those feelings disappeared one night when he counseled with Mary Ann, a warm and attractive woman who suddenly made him feel wanted and needed again. "There has never been anyone," thought Ike, with tears in his eyes, "who cared so much for me and with whom I can share so deeply. I don't think I can go on in life without her."

Late one night after a church council meeting his tortured thoughts ran through his dilemma for the thousandth time. "I love my wife and my children, but I can't live without the warmth and affection of the one who really cares for me as a person." Ike also knew that in his church body ministerial "divorce" is spelled ministerial "DISASTER."

In mental turmoil Pastor Ike headed for Mary Ann, the one person in whose arms he could find peace and security. She wasn't at home, but he found her at a nearby tavern, drunk, and in the arms of another man.

Ike *threw up* in the alley on the way home. He was full of anger at himself. Shame, emptiness and despair set in. But in the morning light he cried through his prayers and thanked God for an experience which had saved him from self-imposed disaster!

The parishioners didn't realize the lesson he had learned, but they noticed the difference in Pastor Ike. Some of the old stiffness and self-righteousness was gone, and they sensed a new compassion coming through his sermons. It was a "tough love" which Ike had mercifully learned from the "tough love" of the Chief Pastor.

God's love has a "penetration" quality that looks beyond your own "unique malfunctions" and loves you as you are. God breaks through your "hard shell" of sin and behind your false bravado. God finds you cold, wet, lonely, trembling and afraid. Piece by piece, God chips away the shell so you can be free from its grasp and be held in the warmth of God's hand. There, nestled in God's love, you can forget the terror of the darkness and bask in the security of the Shepherd's touch. But God's love doesn't stop with the "rescue." Feeding and strengthening you, our Lord teaches you by example that you were designed for more than "rest in the nest." As spiritual energies grow, the Lord calls you to *fly* . . . and to *soar* . . . and to *live!* When one day in your nest you hear the sounds of "new life" struggling in another shell, it's God calling you to look beyond the irritation of the noise and threat of the competition and penetrate the shell to aid in giving "new life." To this you are called and empowered in the forgiving love of Jesus Christ — the Master Pastor!

Paul of Tarsus learned the "Pastor Principle." So did Peter, in Pilate's courtyard. Moses learned it in the wilderness and Ezekiel in a strange and foreign land. Luke saw it demonstrated in his traveling companion, while Mary discovered it looking up from the base of Golgotha! They were all taught by God!

"The Pastor Principle" isn't learned in "navel gazing," "leadership training," "internal analysis," "human encounters," or "touch-and-go sessions." It is "fitted and molded" in the struggle between the twin realities described in Romans 7 . . . "the good that I would I do not and the evil that I would not . . . that I do . . . and who shall deliver me? Thanks be to *God,* through Jesus Christ our Lord!" The "Pastor Principle" is apprehended in the Life and Spirit of the pages of the Scriptures, in the howls of the newborn, at the bedside of the dying, on the trips to the cemetery, in the curses of the ignorant and salty tears of suffering, in the fires of conflict, in the agony of personal repentance and in the *peace* of faith in the Christ of Calvary . . . and Joseph's empty tomb! God speaks to you through the Son! God is there in the frustration, the hard days, the agonizing weeks, the methodical months. Knowing that, experiencing it, *believing God,* there is power to resist the urge to defend yourself when others heap blame, guilt and perverted forms of ecclesiastical garbage on you. Being grasped by the strong right arm of Christ's love, there is courage to confront them with the ultimate strength, "tough love," that penetrating, strengthening, compassionate mercy renewed daily in Jesus Christ! "We love because he first loved us!" (1 John 4:19)

Pastors, take a lesson from the penguins! They can't afford to deny reality and live in a dream world, or they would freeze to death in the icy wastelands of Antarctica. Together with their "dignified companions," they have worked out strategies to *stay alive* and to care for their young. Despite the icy winds that rage down from those crystal mountains, they stand with their friends with a certain "alien dignity" that comes from elsewhere.

Stand tall, then, like penguins! Grow into a maturity that finds its true dignity in "things that are above, not from things on the earth." (Colossians 3) The love of God for you, in Jesus Christ, just as you are, gives you that "alien dignity." God named you and calls you his own. (Isaiah 43:1-3) Though you alone know how weak and vacillating you are, let God stiffen your backbone with "tough love" so that you can show "tough love" to your fellow-believers, despite the icy winds of reality of life in the parish.

As that love is received and passed on, your accusers are overcome! They cannot succeed! As God's love bombards them, their defenses crumble, their accusations lose their force, their tongues are turned to rubber, their ears are uncorked, their eyes dampened and their stony hearts are massaged to life! That's the explosive quality of the ultimate power, "tough love," "The Pastor Principle."

THE ULTIMATE PRINCIPLE FOR PASTORS IS A "TOUGH LOVE" THAT LOOKS BEYOND THE IRRITATION OF THE MOMENT AND IN THE STRENGTH OF CHRIST LOVES PEOPLE AS THEY ARE!

Items for Reflection/Study/Action

Do you agree with the principle, the ultimate strength of "tough love"? Do you see any difference between this and the way "love" has often been construed in the church and world? Is this a fair and accurate translation of the covenant concept of God's "steadfast love" that the Psalm writers spoke of and Christ embodied?

Can you smile as you read about God's "tough love" for you? Have you soaked in some of it lately? How will you be sure to continue to get some? What "filling station" do you have for the nurturing and maturing of your own heart and soul? When do you take time to pray, meditate, let the word speak to you? What devotional aids have you found helpful? Do you have a "father confessor"? Could you have one? What have the veterans in ministry taught you? Have you chosen a favorite "Church Father" to model? Have you found any new resources for ministry lately? Do you know another cleric who would listen and benefit from sharing your resource? After having read all of these principles could you bring yourself to tell him/her? Did you identify with any of those very real experiences and/or feelings? How is this principle working out in your ministry?

Do you remember the reasons you wanted to be a pastor? Were you looking for appreciation, a sense of importance, or a chance to be paid for being "well liked?" Have there been some ingredients in the holy ministry you weren't expecting?

The Pastor Principle can help you to find an even greater benefit than you were looking for, the fulfillment and satisfaction of a life walked in the footsteps of the "Suffering Servant." Surely Jesus too suffered pastoral pain. His tough love enabled Him to say "Father, forgive them for they know not what they do." As God gives us the ability to use "tough love" in our relationships with people, it brings us more meaning in ministry than we ever dreamed of finding!

Perhaps this book has "tweaked" you too hard! If so, we're truly sorry for that. We meant no harm by our style or stance. We just wanted to get your attention. We know how hard it is to break the traditional images of the church and ministry! It's as though they have been insulated or inocculated against reality! The ideal church and the real church are often miles apart! Would you agree? It surely is worth discussing! Whom will you talk with? When?

If you disagree with the way we have written about "maturity in ministry," or with some of the examples we have used, that's fine! We understand disagreements about ministry! However, *please don't disregard what the six principles have to say!* Re-read the preface. Check out the reality of these principles at a future pastoral conference. Share these aspects of ministry with your Council or church officers. It will be beneficial for you and all future parish pastors! We're convinced!

The need for the "reality therapy" that these principles contain has not lessened in our increasingly "religious" society. In fact, we believe that times of religious revival increase the need for something like the *Penguin Principles*. A "ministry to ministers" in the local congregation, by all the people of God, instead of at the distant retreat center, will produce enduring rewards and refreshing maturity for those in the parsonage, pulpit and pew.

How do you feel about that? Could this series of principles be of value to you personally? Can you "try them on for size"? How will you go about it? When will you start? Who will know? Will you need the help of others? Remember the Penguin Principles and waddle off into the fray!

ONE: DESPITE THE PIOUS THINGS WE SAY, AT ANY GIVEN TIME, LESS THAN FIVE PERCENT OF ANY GROUP OF PEOPLE IN THE CHURCH IS OPERATING WITH PURELY CHRISTIAN MOTIVATION. THE OTHER NINETY—FIVE PERCENT IS ASKING, "WHAT'S IN IT FOR ME?"

TWO: MOST OF THE TIME, IN THE WORLD OF THE CHURCH, THINGS ARE NOT WHAT THEY APPEAR TO BE!

THREE: THERE IS A FRICTION IN THE CHURCH THAT BURNS UP ENORMOUS ENERGY, CONSUMES ENDLESS HOURS,

SMOTHERS CREATIVITY, IMPEDES PROGRESS AND OFTEN CRE-
ATES QUITE A LITTLE HEAT!

FOUR: IN THE MINISTRY IT IS BETTER NOT TO KNOW SOME

THINGS, EVEN IF YOU HAVE
TO FORGET THEM FORCE-
FULLY!

FIVE: THEY'LL ONLY DO IT
TO YOU IF YOU LET 'EM!

SIX: THE ULTIMATE
WEAPON FOR PASTORS IS A
"TOUGH LOVE" THAT LOOKS
BEYOND THE IRRITATION OF
THE MOMENT AND, IN THE
STRENGTH OF CHRIST,

LOVES PEOPLE AS THEY ARE.

"The grace of our Lord Jesus Christ, the love of God and the fol-
lowship of the Holy Spirit be with you!"